MORE ʼ____ ᴧ

CONQUERORS

HERBERT BOYD MCGONIGLE

MA BD DD PhD

Former Lecturer at Nazarene Theological College, Dene Road,
Didsbury, Manchester, in the classes in Church History, Theology
Theology and Wesley Studies, Former Principal of Nazarene
Theological for 18 years and now Principal Emeritus

British Library Cataloguing in Publication Data.
A catalogue record for this book is available from the British Library

ISBN 978 0 86071 829 1

A Commissioned Publication Printed by

MOORLEYS
Print, Design & Publishing
info@moorleys.co.uk • www.moorleys.co.uk

Contents

Preface

More than fifty years have gone into this production. I have gathered more than seventy illustrations for this book and I often feel that now is a good time for production it. Jeanne always told me that I should start and now, after three years when she is gone, I have kept my pen handy and now, after fifty years, the time is ready. I was converted in 1955 and a year later I began preaching. I entered the Nazarene College in Scotland and three years on, I was sent to Walthamstow Nazarene Church in London. My first writing was there and I began writing up notes and illustrations. Later, with Jeanne and the children, I left Walthamstow and moved to Uddingston Church of the Nazarene, Glasgow, and after six years, we moved to Leeds Nazarene Church and then to the college in Manchester. For thirty years I taught Church History, Wesley Studies and Theology. For fifty one years I was preaching across Britain and Ireland, the USA and Japan. Later I was to become Principal and taught there for eighteen years. I loved the work - but preaching was my one desire!

I have gathered seventy five readings and more than anyone else, John Wesley is named (!) closely followed by the names of Charles Wesley, John Newton, William Booth, Henry Lyte, Phillip Brookes, William Grimshaw, Joseph Scriven, Samuel Cadman, Samuel Chadwick, and many more. I have given a page or more and six or seven have been my limit. Please enjoy this book and I hope that reading it will do you good and I hope that it will draw you closer to Jesus Christ, our Lord and Saviour.

1. He Cared For The Likes Of Us

These words were spoken by a former prostitute in tribute to the life and ministry of General William Booth, founder of the Salvation Army. Booth was born in Nottingham in 1829 and converted at the age of fifteen. He became a minister in the Methodist New Connexion Church and, together with his wife Catherine, had an outstanding pastorate in Gateshead in Co. Durham.

When his denomination wanted to restrict his itinerant ministry, he left the New Connexion and founded the Christian Mission in London's East End. In 1878 this vigorous evangelistic movement was re-named the 'Salvation Army.' Its workers adopted uniforms, began to use popular music in their services and Booth was named 'General.'

For the next 34 years, Booth led the Salvation Army in aggressive evangelism and social work all over the world. Booth and his Salvation Army 'soldiers,' both men and women, not only preached the gospel of salvation in Christ but resisted social evils of every kind. They organised opposition against drink, gambling and child prostitution. They set up night shelters for the homeless, organised farm colonies, a legal aid service for the poor and a Missing Persons bureau. All over the world the Salvationists' uniform became the badge of those who faithfully preached the gospel and cared for the poor.

William Booth led this great crusade from its inception until his death. In his latter years, he became a national figure respected by everyone. In June 1904 he was granted a private audience with King Edward VII. But no amount of fame and national acclaim could divert Booth from the work of God. He cared for the spiritually lost; he cared for children; he cared for the poor; he cared for those forgotten by society.

He died on August 21st, 1912, and the nation mourned his loss. For three days his body lay in its coffin at Clapton's Congress Hall in London and more than 150,000 filed past in silent respect. His funeral service was held at Olympia's large exhibition hall and records show that 40,000 people attended.

Among the mourners was Britain's Queen Mary, attending incognito the funeral of the man she admired so much. As the cortège passed up the aisle the Queen noticed a shabbily dressed woman place three red carnations on the coffin. Later she asked the woman why she had done this. Not knowing she was speaking to the Queen, the woman confessed she had been a prostitute until she found salvation in Jesus through the Salvation Army's ministry. With tears in her eyes and choking back her emotions, the woman said, 'You see, ma'am, he cared for the likes of us.'

Tributes to William Booth's life and work poured in from all over the world. Heads of state, Church leaders, civic dignitaries and those involved in many kinds of social services all joined to pay their tributes to Booth's life of service for others. But the words spoken to the Queen by the former prostitute were, in many ways, the most eloquent tribute of all. 'He cared for the likes of us.' William Booth believed, and practised, that Christianity is not only the love of God but the love of neighbour as well.

2. Be Still And Know That I Am God

In his Sermon on the Mount, our Lord said, 'Blessed are those who hunger and thirst for righteousness for they will be satisfied' (Matt. 5:6).

These words that link hunger and thirst with blessedness sound strange in our ears. Every night around the world millions of people go to bed hungry and wake up to another day of not knowing where the next meal is coming from. Blessed? Hardly! It is shocking and obscene when we are told the grim facts about world poverty and then told that the average family in Britain wastes £400 of good food every year. But of course our Lord was not talking about physical hunger and thirst on this occasion, although the world's hunger grieves him deeply and he expects that we and all his people will do all we can to relieve it. Rather he was talking about spiritual hunger and spiritual thirst.

We are truly blessed when we long for righteousness. 'Righteousness' is one of the very important words in the Bible. It describes what God is; God is righteous, meaning He is holy, just and absolutely dependable. We are blessed when we long to be like God – when we hunger and thirst to reflect His character in our lives.

When we look into the Scriptures, we see that this longing for God and his likeness is the mark of the saints in every age. It is very prominent in the books of Psalms.

Here is Psalm 42. 'As a hart longs for flowing streams, so longs my soul for you, O God. My souls thirsts for God, for the living God' (vv.1,2). The same longing is expressed in Psalm 63. 'O God, you are my God, I seek you. My soul thirsts for you as in a dry and weary land where no water is' (v.1). When the Psalmist is confronted with the enigmas of life, especially when the wicked seems to triumph, of one thing he is sure. 'Whom have I in heaven but you? There is nothing upon earth that I desire beside you' (Ps. 73:25).

One of the most familiar and most moving expressions of a pilgrim seeking after God is found in Psalm 84. 'My soul longs, even faints, for the courts of the Lord; my heart and my flesh cry out for the living God' (vv.1,2).

This longing for God is not confined to the Old Testament. In Philippians 3 Paul gives us a long autobiographical passage. He tells us what he used to be, what happened to him through meeting with 'Christ Jesus my Lord' – and now what the great all-absorbing ambition of his life is. 'That I may know him and the power of his resurrection' (v.10).

Down through the centuries of the Church it has been the same; the mark of God's people is their longing to know Him and be in closer communion with Him. This longing fills the pages of the biographies and autobiographies of God's servants; from Augustine to Thomas Aquinas, to Martin Luther, to John Wesley, to Elizabeth Fry, to Mother Teresa.

But of course this longing for God is not the prerogative of well-known Christians in the history of the Church; it is the hallmark of all God's people whether expressed publicly or only secretly in prayer. And to all of them, and to us, our Lord gives the most wonderful assurance. When we hunger and thirst to be like him, we will be satisfied!

3. Praying About The Unknown Future

Gen. 15:2-3. 'O Lord God, what will you give me, for I continue childless, and the heir of my house is Eliezer of Damascus?' This is the Bible's first prayer. That doesn't mean that no one before Abraham had prayed but this is the first time we have a record of some praying to God.

We learn as early as Genesis 4 that 'men began to call on the name of the Lord' (v.26) but it does not explicitly say that they prayed. We can hardly believe that godly men like Enoch and Noah never prayed. Enoch 'walked with God' and in his long pilgrimage of 300 years of fellowship with God (Gen. 5:22), he must have prayed many times.

Even before Abraham's first prayer is mentioned, we are told that God appeared to him, that he built an altar for sacrifice and worship and that he called on the name of the Lord (Gen. 12;7; 13:18). But now he faces a real crisis in his life. When God first appeared to him, he had been promised that from his family a great nation would emerge (Gen. 12:1-3). Now many years later he still has no children and custom dictates that his chief servant, Eliezer, will inherit everything. Has God forgotten him? Were all those promises of being a father just make believe or self-delusion? So he cried to God, 'What will you give me?'

It was a desperate prayer from a desperate heart. What was God doing? Why had He not kept His promises? Had He forgotten? Was He not able to do what He had promised? We have all been where Abraham was when he prayed that prayer. We want to believe but why is nothing happening?

Then God answered! 'Your own son shall be your heir' (v.4). This wonderful answer was sealed with a dramatic illustration. God directed Abraham to look up into the night sky. 'Number the stars if you can,' God said. 'So shall your descendants be.' Abraham would have as many offspring as the stars in the sky! Impossible? Incredible? Far-fetched? But it happened!

5

The next chapter records the birth of his son Ishmael and two chapters later we read of the birth of Isaac, the son of promise. And history, both biblical and secular, confirms that the illustration from the stars was no exaggeration!

So the Bible's first prayer helps us in a number of ways. First, when our hearts ache because of fear or doubt or uncertainty, take it to God in prayer. Second, God's delays are not denials. Third, with Abraham who 'believed the Lord' (v.6), trust quietly in our sovereign and gracious God.

4. A Thousand Tongues!

Following his evangelical heart-warming experience of May 21st 1738, Charles Wesley was totally committed both to preaching the gospel and hymn-writing. In the next few years, hundreds of hymns came from his pen and some of them were destined to be among the most popular he ever wrote. His 'Conversion Hymn,' written on May 22nd 1738, laid a pattern of expounding Scripture in lyrical verse that would characterise his hymns for the next fifty years. That first hymn opened with a declaration of the wonder, the surprise, the sheer joy of the new-born soul!

> Where shall my wondering soul begin?
> How shall I all to heaven aspire?
> A slave redeemed from death and hell
> A brand plucked from the eternal fire…

It was quickly followed by a hymn entitled 'Free Grace.' It echoed the theme of a sermon preached and published by his brother John Wesley in which God's saving grace in Christ was announced as 'free in all and free for all.' Salvation is by grace alone and that grace reaches out to all the world. Charles' verses quickly established themselves as one of his all-time best loved hymns.

> And can it be that I should gain
> An interest in the Saviour's blood?

On the morning of his conversion day, he had read Martin Luther's commentary on Galatians 2. When he came to v. 20 he was particularly struck with the words, 'the Son of God who loved me and gave himself for me.' In his commentary, Luther advised the reader to 'read these words "me" and "my" with great emphasis.' So Charles did, and read, 'He loved *me* and gave himself for *me.*' In that moment the Spirit illuminated the great scripture doctrine of Christ's sacrificial death for sinners, and in that moment Charles, in his own words, found himself 'at peace with God.'

Charles Wesley had learned from the New Testament that saving faith is not just a general belief in Christ; rather it is faith in His atoning death and resurrection. It is faith in the mighty work Christ wrought on the Cross. This Pauline theology, especially as found in his letters to the Romans and the Galatians, comes out in this hymn. Charles captures Paul's amazement in the words, 'He loved me and gave himself for me.'

Died He for *me* who caused His pain
For *me* who Him to death pursued?
Amazing love! How can it be
That Thou, my God, shouldst die for *me*?

Charles then follows with some wonderful descriptions of Christ's Incarnation and Atonement. 'He left His Father's throne above.' 'Emptied Himself of all but love.' 'Tis mystery all, the Immortal dies. He bled for Adam's helpless race.' 'Tis mercy all, immense and free.' Free grace indeed! And it is personal, 'For, O my God, it found out *me*'!! Then follows the graphic account of his own hour of spiritual birth – in words that multitudes of Christians can identify with. Using the story of Peter's imprisonment recorded in Acts 4, Charles describes the sinner as 'bound in sin and nature's night.' But Christ comes by His Spirit and the miracle happens!

Thine eye diffused a quickening ray
I woke, the dungeon flamed with light.
My chains fell off, my heart was free
I rose, went forth, and followed Thee.

In Romans Paul speaks about the believer in Christ being free from condemnation (8:1). Charles picks up this truth to write his climactic verse.

No condemnation now I dread
Jesus, and all in Him, is mine
Alive in Him my living Head ...

While the hymn, '*And can it be?*' was written sometime in the months following May 1738, another of Charles' most popular hymns can be dated precisely. Published in 1739, it was entitled, 'A Hymn for the Anniversary Day of one's Conversion,' and it was meant as a thanksgiving for May 21 1738. The opening lines are:

Glory to God, and praise, and love
Be ever, ever given....

All editions of this hymn found in modern hymnbooks begin with verse 7.

O for a thousand tongues to sing
My great Redeemer's praise
The glories of my God and King
The triumphs of His grace!

Charles wrote 18 verses for this hymn but hymnbooks use at most seven or eight of the stanzas. Charles longs to tell the good news of the gospel to others. He asks God for help in order,

To spread through all the earth abroad
The honours of Thy name.

With his own heart warmed with the redeeming love of God, he proclaims the beauty and glory and saving power of the name of Jesus. It's the name that 'charms our fears;' it 'bids our sorrows cease;' it is 'music in the sinner's ears;' it brings 'life and health and peace.' As the New Testament teaches, Christ alone can forgive our sins and set us spiritually free.

He breaks the power of cancelled sin
He sets the prisoner free
His blood can make the foulest clean
His blood availed for me.

The hymn echoes God's invitation in Isaiah 45:22. 'Look to me and be saved, all the ends of the earth.'

Look unto Him, ye nations; own
Your God, ye fallen race …

See all your sins on Jesus laid
The Lamb of God was slain
His soul was once an offering made
For every soul of man.

Charles Wesley's hymns emphasised especially what might be called the doctrines of grace. These included hymns on universal sin, our inability to save ourselves, the reality of death and judgement, the atonement made by Christ's death and resurrection, saving faith, the new birth and the assurance of salvation by the Holy Spirit. As the Cross of Christ is central to the gospel, Charles wrote hymn after hymn on this great theme. In 1749, in a hymn entitled 'Invitation to Sinners,' he wrote of Christ as the one who paid our ransom.

> All ye that pass by
> To Jesus draw nigh
> To you is it nothing that Jesus should die?
> Your Ransom and Peace
> Your Surety He is
> Come, see if there ever was sorrow like His.

Preaching the gospel of salvation by faith in Jesus Christ is the glorious calling of all God's servants. As Charles Wesley gave thanks to God for His blessing on his own ministry, he encouraged all preachers to proclaim the Good News.

> Ye servants of God
> Your master proclaim
> And publish abroad
> His wonderful name.
> The name all victorious
> Of Jesus extol
> His Kingdom is glorious
> And rules over all.

In that same year, 1749, he composed a hymn of twenty-two verses that glorified Jesus as Lord and Saviour. It became another of his most popular hymns.

> Jesus the Name high over all
> In hell, or earth, or sky
> Angels and men before it fall
> And devils fear and fly.

Charles Wesley's delight in being a preacher of the gospel finds lyrical expression in the final verse.

> Happy, if with my latest breath
> I might but gasp His name
> Preach Him to all, and cry in death
> Behold! Behold the Lamb!

There seemed to be no end to Charles Wesley's poetic inspiration! Year after year hundreds and hundreds of hymns flowed from his warmed heart and his immersion in Scripture. While many are not known today, some have a place among the most popular hymns in the English language. These include, 'Jesus, Lover of my soul;' 'O for a heart to praise my God;' 'Christ the Lord is risen today;' 'Arise, my soul, arise.'

Charles Wesley was at his poetic best when writing hymns on the Cross of Christ. He was pre-eminently the poet of redemption. In 1747 he published a collection of fifty-two hymns under the general title, 'Hymns for those that seek and those that have Redemption in the Blood of Jesus Christ.' One of these hymns was based on the parable of the Great Supper (Luke 14:16-24) and opened with words of invitation.

> Come, sinners to the gospel feast
> Let every soul be Jesu's guest …
> The love of God in Christ reaches out to all the world and the invitation includes us all.
>
> Sent by my Lord, on you I call
> The invitation is to all
> Come all the world, come, sinner, thou
> All things in Christ are ready now.

Another invitation hymn began:

> Weary souls that wander wide
> From the central point of bliss
> Turn to Jesus crucified
> Fly to those dear wounds of His …

In this collection there was one hymn that would gain universal popularity. While today it is a very popular wedding hymn, Charles Wesley meant it to express the love of God for a lost world; the love that moved Him to send His Son to be the Saviour (John 3:16).

> Love Divine, all loves excelling
> Joy of heaven to earth come down …

As Jesus our Saviour is 'pure, unbounded love,' so the hymn prays:
> Visit us with Thy salvation
> Enter every trembling heart.

As every Christian is called and empowered by the Holy Spirit to live a holy life, so the final verse invokes the Lord to carry on His great work of transformation in us.
> Finish then Thy new creation
> Pure and spotless let us be ...

Paul wrote that in Christ the Christian is 'being changed into His likeness from one degree of glory to another' (2 Cor. 3:18). Charles Wesley takes this theme of glory to glory and sees it as describing the Christian's pilgrimage to the 'final glory' – standing in Christ's presence for ever!
> Changed from glory into glory
> Till in heaven we take our place
> Till we cast our crowns before Thee
> Lost in wonder, love and praise

5. He Wanted Something Better

Jesus Christ came into the world to save sinners (1 Tim. 1:15). That one sentence summarises the whole life and death and resurrection of our Lord. He came into our world to save sinners – a wonderful, simple, clear and glorious gospel.

This sentence from Paul is vividly illustrated by James Stalker (1848-1927), a Scottish scholar and university lecturer. One of the outstanding evangelical preachers of his day, Stalker published two very famous books, the *Life of Christ* and the *Life of St Paul*. He followed this up some years later with an extended treatment of Christ's last days on earth; *The Trial and Death of Jesus Christ*. Subtitled 'A Devotional History of our Lord's Passion,' it is a scholarly, exegetical and devotional account of the last week of Christ's life. In the book Stalker relates how Paul's words were illustrated in an incident that happened many years earlier.

While he was a student at Edinburgh University, he went one day to visit a man who was dying in early life. This man had also been an Edinburgh student and had graduated with great academic distinction. He had gone to teach in a colonial university and in a few years was made a professor. His academic prospects looked brilliant and then, suddenly, he was struck down with an incurable disease. He came back home to Scotland to die.

On the day that Stalker visited the dying man, some other friends had come to take him for a drive in a carriage. On the return journey, he asked Stalker to sit beside him. He said the other friends had been very kind and had read to him long passages from Thomas Carlyle's celebrated book, *Sartor Resartus*. 'But,' said the dying man, 'I am so awfully tired of it.'

This outstanding scholar was a great admirer of the book, but now, with death not far away, he wanted something better. Stalker tells how the sick man looked him straight in the eye and began to repeat with great solemnity, 'This is a faithful saying, and worthy of all acceptation, that Jesus Christ came into the world to save sinners, of whom I am chief.' Then he added with great simplicity. 'There is nothing else of any use to me now.'

The great literature of the world has much to teach us but the Bible is in a class by itself. The Bible alone tells us that God loved us and sent His Son Jesus Christ to die for us. As Dr Stalker pointed out, the dying man was a great literary expert but as he neared death, he turned again to the Bible. In his own words, nothing else was of any use as he faced the grave. And how appropriate was the passage he quoted from memory! 'Christ Jesus came into the world to save sinners …' In living and in dying, the gospel of Calvary is still 'the old, old story, of Jesus and His love.'

6. The Hopes And Fears Of All The Years

These words come from Phillip Brooks' familiar Christmas hymn, 'O little town of Bethlehem.' In four lines Brooks' reminds us that in the birth of Jesus the salvation of the world was being played out in Bethlehem.

> In thy dark street shineth
> The everlasting Light
> The hopes and fears of all the years
> Are met in thee tonight.

More and more these days people are asking if the Christmas story has any meaning and if it has any relevance. Some Christians even say that the New Testament doesn't tell us to celebrate Christmas so we should drop the whole event from the Church calendar.

The word 'Christmas' comes from the old Anglo-Saxon; from 'Christ' and from 'masse' meaning 'mass' or 'celebration.' So the word 'Christmas' means 'Christ's celebration,' and it was because Christians from the earliest times believed that Christ was God incarnate that His birth was celebrated.

Even though we can't be sure of the exact month of His birth, much less the exact day, yet His coming into the world was such a mighty event that the instinct to celebrate it is in harmony with the New Testament. Even the calendar reminds us of His coming for we divide history into the time before His coming, BC, and the time since His coming, AD.

In three verses in Luke's Gospel, the meaning of Christmas is spelt out so simply and so vividly. Luke gives us the Christmas Message. 'Don't be afraid. I bring you good news of great joy... For all the people. There is born to you today a Saviour, who is Christ the Lord' (2:10,11).

Luke's words still thrill us with their timeless good news! We need only look at some of his key words and phrases. 'Don't be afraid ... I bring good news... great joy... for all the people.' Nothing in our

15

world this Christmas can compare with that! No need to be fearful! The news is good! There is great joy for all who will believe it! And then he tells us what the good news is. A Saviour is born! He is Christ the Lord!

But as well as this Christmas Message Luke has a Christmas Miracle for us! 'This will be the sign to you: You will find a baby.' God's answer to the needs of the world was to send a baby! People everywhere were looking for a deliverer, perhaps another Moses; for a king coming in the glory and splendour of a Solomon; for a potentate like Cyrus to bring peace to the nations; for a long-promised Messiah. And God sent a baby! A baby, yes, but this Baby was the Incarnate God!

And Luke has one more word, for to the Christmas Message and Miracle he adds the Christmas Mission. 'The Dayspring ...has visited us to give light to those who sit in darkness and the shadow of death, and to guide our feet in the way of peace' (1:78, 79). The Dayspring is the gentle light of the rising sun. Christ our Lord came into our world silently and gently like the coming of the dawn, for had He come in all His ineffable glory and majesty we would have been blinded. And He came to bring the light of the love and mercy of God to us lost sinners and to guide us in the way of peace. And all who believe this grand and glorious gospel will celebrate His Coming this Christmas!

7. The Prophets Chamber

Church History tells us a lot about what happened in England's 18th century Revival. We know about John and Charles Wesley, George Whitefield, the formation of the 'Methodist Societies' and much, much else. But how did this Revival affect ordinary families?

A wonderful account from Cornwall gives us some answers. In August 1743, two of John Wesley's preachers asked for shelter in a home in the village of Trewint, some eight miles south-west of Launceston. Before they left next morning the two men paid for the hospitality and then asked the woman of the house if they could pray. To her great surprise, as she told her husband later, 'they prayed without a book.'

Some weeks later John Nelson, one of the two preachers, returned to the cottage. The owners, Digory and Elizabeth Isbell, warmly welcomed him. The next morning Nelson preached on their doorstep and the couple were profoundly moved. As Nelson wrote in his journal: 'The man and his wife who received us received the Lord who sent us.' Salvation had come to the Isbell home.

Seven months later Digory and Elizabeth gave a warm welcome to John Wesley himself. Rejoicing in their new-found faith, they felt so privileged to have the famous preacher in their humble cottage. Digory had announced Wesley's coming to his neighbours and that evening Wesley preached to 'more people than the house could contain.' Later, leaving Cornwall after two weeks of itinerant preaching, Wesley was back with the Isbells and what an occasion it was! Their third child, Hannah, had just been born and this was the day of her baptism. It just so happened that George Whitefield was there also and Hannah Isbell was baptised by England's two great evangelists! How often in the coming years that story would be told of how John Wesley, assisted by George Whitefield and two local clergymen, baptised the infant girl in Altarnun parish church.

And so the Isbell home became the lodging place for the Methodist evangelists and preachers entering and leaving Cornwall. One day as he read his Bible, Digory read the story in 2 Kings 4 of how the woman in Shunem entertained the prophet Elisha and later furnished a room for 'the man of God.' Digory, a stonemason by profession, was fired with enthusiasm by this story. He set to and built an addition to his cottage home – a room ten feet square, furnished with a bed, a table and a stool. A prophet's chamber indeed!

Throughout the Isbells' lifetime, and for many years after, scores of travelling preachers were made welcome in that hallowed place. The cottage was a centre for the Methodist work in that part of Cornwall, for Digory and Elizabeth, like so many in those days, became fervent Methodists while remaining loyal members of their local parish church. And the Isbell cottage still stands there today and is now a Methodist museum and open to the public. On its doorstep the gospel was preached many times and its old walls resounded often to fervent Methodist singing. Like Lydia long ago when she heard Paul preach, Digory and Elizabeth Isbell had opened their hearts to the Lord. Then they opened their home to God's servants and so their names live on in the records of the men and women of true faith.

8. Faithful And Wise Stewards

In the New Testament all Christians are reminded and encouraged to be good stewards. So Peter writes, 'As each has received a gift, employ it for one another as good stewards of God's varied grace' (1 Pet. 4:10). As Christians we are called to use wisely and responsibly whatever gifts and abilities God has given to us. This is made very clear in what is usually called our Lord's parable of the 'talents' (Matt. 25:14-30). Each of the three servants was given a sum of money. Later they were asked to report on their stewardship, on how they had used the gifts entrusted to them. Luke records that Jesus taught his disciples the importance of diligent service. 'Who then is the faithful and wise steward whom his master will set over his household?' (Lk. 12:42).

An illustration of faithful stewardship comes from the life and ministry of Dr Adam Clarke (1760-1832). Clarke is widely known because of his commentary on the whole Bible. He spent 30 years on his commentary and it became one of the most popular evangelical commentaries of the 19th and 20th centuries. Although a full-time Wesleyan preacher, Clarke was a prodigious scholar who worked easily in at least ten languages! What is amazing about Clarke's scholarship is that he was self-taught! Shortly after his teenage conversion in a field near his home in Co Londonderry, North Ireland, Clarke went off to John Wesley's school in Kingswood, Bristol. He was there only a very short time when Wesley recognised his preaching gifts and appointed him to his first preaching circuit.

But while he was at Kingswood, something happened that affected the rest of his life. He was sent to dig the garden to pay for his keep and one day his spade turned up a half-guinea. No one claimed the coin so the headmaster gave it to Clarke to keep. The half guinea was equal to ten and a half shillings, a little more than half a pound sterling and was a small fortune in the 1780s. Clarke often said later that he almost spent the half guinea buying the clothes he needed, and food to supplement the school's very meagre fare.

But Adam Clarke didn't spend the money on food or clothing; instead he spent most of it on buying a recently-published Hebrew grammar! From it he acquired an excellent knowledge of the Hebrew language and this whetted his appetite for more. In the subsequent years he mastered Arabic, Aramaic, Persian, Greek, Latin, French, Spanish, German, etc.

When the British and Foreign Bible Society (now the Bible Society) was formed in 1804, Clarke was a committee member. He was personally responsible for editing and publishing the Society's first Persian New Testament. In more than fifty years of preaching, translating and publishing, Clarke devoted all his linguistic skills to promoting the gospel of Christ. His commentary on the Bible has blessed generations of readers. All this amazing output of scholarship can be traced back to the day he used most of his half-guinea to buy a Hebrew grammar. What fruitful stewardship! We may not have the gifts of languages and learning that Adam Clarke had. If, however, we devote what gifts and talents God has given to us entirely to His work and glory, He will use them. We can all be 'faithful and wise stewards.'

9. The Gospel of the Warmed Heart

The Revd John Wesley (1703-91) began preaching in 1725, the year of his ordination and he continued to be a preacher for 66 years.

In May 1738 something very significant happened in his life that both changed him dramatically and the direction of his life. He had returned to England after spending two frustrating years as a missionary to the American Indians. On the homeward journey he had written a kind of spiritual memorandum in which he spoke of his disappointments and spiritual depression. He had gone to Georgia to convert the heathen, but, he asked, 'who will convert me'? He was a dedicated, orthodox, Bible-believing churchman, yet something was missing in his life. There was no joy, no sense of the presence of God, no inner witness of the Spirit that his own sins were forgiven. In London he met a young Moravian missionary, Peter Bohler, who witnessed to him, and his brother Charles, about personal saving faith. Bohler wisely advised Wesley to continue preaching according to the conviction and light that God had already given him, assuring him that God would soon answer his fears and doubts.

And Bohler was right! On Wednesday evening, May 24th 1738, John Wesley sat in a gathering of dedicated Christian people meeting in Aldersgate Street in London. The leader read from Martin Luther's 'Preface' to his commentary on Romans. As he read Luther's words about how the Holy Spirit creates saving faith in the heart, Wesley recorded. 'I felt my heart strangely warmed. I felt I did trust in Christ, Christ alone, for salvation, and an assurance was given me that He had taken away my sins, even mine, and saved me from the law of sin and death.' A spiritual heart-warming indeed! In his *Journal*, Wesley wrote the words *my*, *mine* and *me* in italics to emphasise how personal that great experience was. Ever since his ordination Wesley had sought this personal assurance but it alluded him for thirteen years. Now he knew for sure that his sins were forgiven, that he was reconciled to God and that the Spirit witnessed with his spirit that he had eternal life.

That heart-warming was the beginning of his life's work as an evangelist. In the next half-century, under his itinerant ministry, thousands of people would find the same experience of spiritual assurance and peace with God. Three days prior to John's life-changing experience, on May 21st 1738, Pentecost Sunday, his brother Charles Wesley had found the same heart-warming transformation by the Spirit. Exactly a year later, Charles wrote a hymn to express praise to God for what had happened to his brother and himself on those memorable days. He entitled it, 'A Hymn for the Anniversary Day of One's Conversion,' and it has been a favourite with Christian people ever since.

> O for a thousand tongues to sing
> My great Redeemer's praise
> The glories of my God and King
> The triumphs of his grace.

10. Praying The Praying Of Forgiveness

Numbers 12:13, 'O God, heal her, I pray.' These six words are Moses' prayer for his sister Miriam. They tell us a lot about Moses and a lot about prayer.

For some time, Miriam and her brother Aaron had been simmering with anger against Moses. They protested that he had married a Cushite woman (v.1), but the real cause of their animosity was jealousy. 'Has the Lord spoken only through Moses?' (v.2). Don't we have a ministry as well? Hasn't God also spoken through us? Why does everyone look to Moses? Why are we overlooked?

Jealousy is a powerful and deadly emotion. God had given ministries and honour to Miriam (Exod. 15:20,21) and Aaron had become the chief priest (Num. 3:1-3), but neither of them were satisfied with that. It looks as if Miriam fomented and took the lead in criticising Moses. Suddenly the Lord intervened (v.4). He called Moses, Aaron and Miriam together and defended his servant Moses. Moses is faithful in all my house! (v.7) Whereas the Lord had often spoken to other prophets in dreams and visions, He speaks to Moses 'mouth to mouth' (v.8). How dare Aaron and Miriam question Moses whom the Lord called 'my servant' (v.8). Having so strongly defended Moses and rebuked his critics, the Lord departed and then the divine judgement fell. Suddenly Miriam, the leader of the conspiracy, was struck down with the dreaded leprosy.

Aaron immediately cried out to Moses, confessing his own and his sister's sin and foolishness (vv. 11,12). Then Moses demonstrated why the Lord honoured him so highly. He expressed no anger, no vindictiveness, no spirit of 'settling scores' against his brother and sister. In spite of their antagonism and jealousy, Moses loved them both and 'cried to the Lord' on behalf of Miriam. He prayed one of the shortest prayers found in the Bible. 'O God, heal her, I pray' (v.13). He was grieved and full of compassion to see his sister so terribly afflicted. The prayer was prompted by the love that forgives, the love that overlooks what others have done to us, the love that wants God's best for them. And only God's grace can make us like that. The prayer is so short, so simple, so direct, so personal. 'O God, heal her, I pray.' And God heard and answered. As a warning to others who might challenge Moses' authority, Miriam was quarantined for seven days, then fully healed and restored (vv.14, 15).

How does this incident help us in our prayer life? First, true prayer is born in compassion. The lips express the deep feelings of the heart. Second, God will not hear our prayers if our hearts are not right with him and with one another. While we cherish resentments and grudges, our praying is powerless. Third, while there are many times when prayer needs to be persistent, there are also times when it is a simple, deep cry from the heart.

11. From White House To Log Cabin

James A Garfield was the 20th President of the United States of America. He was born into a poor family who lived in a log cabin in Orange, Cuyahoga County, Ohio, in November 1831.

His father, Abram Garfield, had an ancestry that was descended from the Pilgrim Fathers. He died at the age of 33, leaving his wife Eliza with five children, of whom James was the youngest.

James went to school at the age of three and went on to an Academy when he was 18. He was a diligent student who went on to Williams College in 1854 and graduated with first-class honours. For the next 25 years, he displayed outstanding talent as a college president, a senator and a major general in the army. He won the Presidential election and was inaugurated as America's 20th President on March 4th 1881. On July 2nd that year, he was mortally wounded by an assassin's bullet and died on September 19th.

That, in a few short paragraphs, is a summary biography of James A Garfield. The full story is told by William Thayer in his book, *From Log Cabin to White House*. It is a famous biography of the fatherless boy who went on from humble beginnings to hold the highest office in the United States of America. It began in a log cabin in the wilderness of Ohio and it ended in the White House in Washington.

At this Christmas season here is a familiar story that's entitled *From White House to Log Cabin*. It is the story of Jesus Christ. Forever with the Father in eternal glory, He left it all and entered our world in a cattle shed in Bethlehem, long, long ago. He who made the worlds was born into ours in a manger. He who shared the ineffable glory of the eternal Trinity 'laid it aside' and wrapped himself in human flesh. In Jesus, God became man and came into this world by the back door. In the moving words of George MacDonald, the Christmas story is about 'a little baby thing that made a woman cry.' But that baby was God incarnate. He split the whole of human history with His coming so that now we speak of BC and AD. He exchanged the glory of heaven for a manger, a cross and finally an empty tomb. His biography is indeed – from *White House to Log Cabin*. He became poor to make many rich! He embraced death to give us life! He left heaven to take us back there with Him! Let us worship the incarnate Saviour. Charles Wesley put it so well.

> *Born* that man no more may die
> *Born* to raise the sons of earth
> *Born* to give them second birth.

12. Celebrating Two Centuries of Freedom

More than 200 years ago, on 25th March 1807, the British Parliament in London voted for a Law that was to have important and far-reaching repercussions around the world in the then far-flung British Empire.

The new Law prohibited all British ships from transporting slaves anywhere on the high seas. Captains who were caught breaking the law would be fined heavily and if the offence was repeated they would lose their shipping license. This Act of 1807 was one of the most humanitarian pieces of legislation ever enacted in the British parliament and it is fitting that 200 years on we recall how it was brought about and what it achieved. What is particularly significant about the 1807 Act is that it was proposed, promoted and carried to a successful conclusion mostly by a small number of very determined Christians.

The British Empire had been deeply involved in the slave traffic since the late 16th century. Men and women were forcibly taken from Africa and transported to British colonies in America and the West Indies.

They were used as slave labour in the tobacco plantations in the New World and on the sugar plantations of the Caribbean. Britain was not alone in her use of slave labour. France, Portugal, Spain and Germany were all involved in this barbarous trade but the increasing size of the British Empire meant that Britain's plantation owners depended more and more on a steady supply of slave labour.

Sir Francis Drake, forever famous in British history for his naval victories over the Spanish, led the way in transporting slaves across the world. His cousin, Sir John Howard, was also a transporter of slaves and both men grew immensely rich from their participation in the business of human misery. The cities of Liverpool and Bristol were the main centres for shipping slaves and in both locations merchants and businessmen made huge personal fortunes from the slave business.

Research has shown that in the two hundred years from 1600 to 1800, no fewer than twelve million black men, women and children were taken by force from Africa and transported as slave labour. This was the largest forced migration of men and women in human history.

While these figures are shocking as a catalogue of human traffic, what cannot be computed is the number of slaves who died on the terrible voyages across the oceans. Locked in chains below decks in conditions of unspeakable squalor and often victims of typhoid, dysentery and other diseases, uncounted thousands died at sea and were promptly dumped overboard. The lives of those poor people snatched from their African homelands were often short, savage and utterly brutal. Even those who lived to reach the plantations were destined to an early death. The forced labour, the lack of care and medicine for the sick and the harsh regime of the 'killing fields' meant that the mortality rate among the slaves was cruelly high. As the slaves died at sea or at work, the slave ships kept up a steady supply of replacement.

While the Act of 1807 was of great significance, an earlier legislation in 1772 had gone some way to give relief to black slaves living in Britain.

Many plantation owners had their homes in Britain and when they returned from abroad, they brought black slaves with them. In 1729 the then Attorney General ruled that 'a slave by coming from the West Indies to Great Britain or Ireland, doth not become free and baptism doth not bestow freedom on him, nor make any alteration to his temporal condition in these kingdoms.' For the next 50 years as many as 12,000 slaves were employed as chattels in the homes of the rich merchants in England and Scotland.

Finally in 1772, in what became the famous Somerset Case, slave owning in the British Isles was abolished. James Somerset was a black slave in the household of Charles Stuart. Having escaped in England, he was recaptured and put on a ship bound for Jamaica. Hearing of

Somerset's plight, the prominent anti-slavery campaigner Granville Sharpe successfully applied for a writ of *habeas corpus*. The ship's captain was ordered to produce Somerset in court where Lord Mansfield, the Lord Chief Justice, ruled that owning a slave in Britain was contrary to law. It was during this trial that Lord Mansfield delivered the famous verdict, 'Let justice be done though the heavens may fall.' James Somerset won his freedom and the outcome was that slave owning in Britain became a crime.

While the Somerset Case was a victory for slaves in Britain, it didn't affect slaves on the high seas or on the plantations. But now other voices were raised in protest and outrage against the British slave traffic. Foremost among the protestors was the Revd John Wesley, leader of the Evangelical Revival. In 1774 he published *Thoughts upon Slavery*, an impassioned attack on the whole foundation and system of slavery in the Empire. Believing that basic Christianity is the love of God and man, Wesley attacked slavery as inhuman and unjust and pilloried those who made money out of the misery of their fellow men and women. Answering those who said that the economics of the British Empire required slave labour, Wesley retorted, 'Better no trade than trade procured by villainy. Better is honest poverty than all the riches bought by the tears, sweat and blood of our fellow creatures.' Against the owners of the plantations Wesley directed his fire. 'The blood of thy brother crieth against thee from the earth, from the ship and from the waters. …Thy hands, thy bed, thy furniture, thy house, thy lands, are at present stained with blood.' Seventeen years later, in 1791, as Wesley lay dying in his house in London, he wrote his last letter, still protesting against the slave trade. It was addressed to William Wilberforce who was about to present another anti-slavery petition in Parliament. Wesley encouraged Wilberforce not to be 'worn out by the opposition of men and devils… Go on, in the name of God …in exposing that execrable villainy, which is the scandal of religion, of England, and of human nature.'

Another voice raised against slavery was that of the Revd John Newton (1725-1807). Captain of a slave ship, Newton was converted in 1747, took holy orders in 1764 and became curate of Olney parish, Buckinghamshire, and finished his ministry as rector of St Mary's Woolnoth in London. In 1788 he published *Thoughts upon the African Slave Trade*, repudiating it as 'the stain of our national character.' The slave trade is 'a poisonous root, diffusing its malignity into every branch.' No commerce was 'so cruel, so oppressive, so destructive, as the African Slave Trade.' Other prominent people in England joined the protest against slavery, including Mary Birkett (1774-1817), a Dublin Quaker, Mary Wollstonecraft (1759-97), campaigner for women's rights, and Josiah Wedgwood (1730-95), the famous Staffordshire potter. Quakers in Britain and America were especially prominent in the campaign to end the slave trade.

It was, however, mainly due to the campaigning of William Wilberforce and his supporters that the momentous Act was finally ratified in the House of Commons in 1807. Wilberforce (1759-1833), was a Cambridge graduate who entered politics at the age of twenty and was converted to personal faith in Christ at the age of twenty-five. He became a member of the Clapham Sect, a remarkable and influential group of evangelical Anglicans who worshipped together at Clapham in south London. This group included Thomas Clarkson (1760-1846), classical scholar and tireless campaigner; Henry Thornton (1760-1815), banker, philanthropist and Member of Parliament; Granville Sharp (1735-1813), scholar and administrator; Hannah More (1745-1835), writer and philanthropist; Thomas Babington (1800-1859), 1st Baron Macaulay and Member of Parliament, and John Venn (1759-1813), rector of Holy Trinity Church, Clapham.

Vilified by much of the public press of the day, and attacked and misrepresented by the promoters of the slave trade, the Clapham Sect devoted its time, money, influence and prayer to a variety of social causes but its attack on slavery in the British Empire was by far its greatest success. Clarkson and Sharp, in particular, travelled far and wide, collecting facts about every aspect of slavery. They produced documentary evidence and harrowing eyewitness accounts of the terrible sufferings endured by the slaves on the long sea voyages and in the plantations of the West Indies.

Supported by his friends inside and outside Parliament, Wilberforce presented his first Abolition Bill in 1783 but was defeated. His second attempt in 1787 was likewise defeated. Undaunted by the influence and manipulation of those who opposed him, and by their virulent personal attacks, Wilberforce continued to gather evidence and lobby Members of Parliament. He was defeated twice again, in 1791 and 1805 but victory was not far away. In February 1806 Lord Grenville formed a Whig administration and he began to campaign in the House of Lords to strengthen the vote against slavery. Wilberforce and Charles Fox, the Foreign Secretary, led the campaign in the House of Commons. When it finally came to a vote on what was called 'the Abolition of the Slave Trade Bill', the House of Lords voted for it by 41 votes to 20 and it was carried in the Commons by 114 votes to 15. The historic Bill became law on 25th March 1807.

Wilberforce and his supporters had brought an end to slaves being transported on British ships but the campaign was not over. In 1823 a Society was formed for the total Abolition of Slavery. Wilberforce died on 29th July 1833. One month later the British Parliament passed the *Slavery Abolition Act*. It granted freedom to all slaves held in the British Empire. The *Act* of 1833 was the winning of the war but the first decisive round was won when Wilberforce and his friends steered the Bill of 1807 to victory.

13. The Prayers For Holy Love

1 Thess. 3:12, 13, 'May the Lord ...establish your hearts unblamable in holiness.' Paul's first letter to the Thessalonian Church, dating from about 51AD, is generally regarded as the first book in the New Testament to have been written. That means that this prayer is the first New Testament prayer to have been composed. Paul has already highly commended the genuine spiritual experience and character of these new Christians. He thanked God for their faith, love and hope, 1:3; they were examples to others, 1:7; their faith in God was being widely spoken about, 1:8; and having turned from idolatry they were now serving the true God and expecting Christ's Second Coming, 1:9, 10. It is for these new and enthusiastic believers that Paul now prays.

The prayer asks for two great blessings for these Christians. First that they may abound in love toward each other and to the world, and then that their conduct will be characterised by holy living. What a model prayer this is for Christians in every age! Note Paul's words, 'may the Lord make you increase and abound in love' (v.12). This is not merely asking that these believers will love one another but that their love will be full and overflowing. Perhaps Paul is recalling that Jesus said the world would recognise His disciples by their love toward one another (John 13:35). But this love, the essence of Christian experience, is not narrow or parochial. Paul prayed that their love would abound not only to each other but also 'to all men.' What a picture of what His Church should be! All of us who claim to be His people should be known by our love for one another and for the world for which He died.

Then comes the second request in the prayer, that their hearts will be 'established unblamable in holiness.' (v.13). The word 'established' translated means to be fixed, to be settled, indicating constant character. In this world no Christian can be faultless but by His grace and mercy we are called to be blameless. In the prayer Paul brings together the condition of our hearts - overflowing in love, and the quality of our conduct - steadfast in holy living. What a combination of holy love, a reflection of what Jesus was!

One other aspect of this prayer is worth noting. When Paul prays that the love of these Christians will abound to each other, he adds that this is how he feels about them; 'as we do to you' (v.12). Likewise in 2:10 Paul says the Thessalonians are witnesses of his holy, righteous and blameless conduct among them. The love and holiness for which Paul prays for these believers can be seen in his own life and work. Surely the most pressing need in all our congregations is that all of us as Christ's disciples will consistently bear witness to His love controlling our hearts and our conduct.

14. John Wesley And The Means Of Grace

John Wesley was no 'hit and run' evangelist. In his half-century of itinerant preaching in Britain, he took the most meticulous care in the 'follow up' work. All those who professed saving faith were taught and encouraged to share in the means of grace daily, weekly and on other occasions. He wrote: 'I determine, by the grace of God, not to strike one stroke in any place where I cannot follow the blow.' He was convinced that when believers are brought to saving faith in Jesus Christ, this is just the beginning of their pilgrimage. And there were two main sources of the means of grace that John Wesley strongly impressed on all his followers. The first was the Sunday service in the local parish church. John Wesley was born into the Church of England and died an ordained minister in that Church. In his lifetime he used all his influence to ensure that his 'Methodist' people were regular communicants in their parish churches. He set a personal example of this kind of devotion. When he was charged with attempting to set up a new denomination, he flatly denied it. 'I dare not renounce communion with the Church of England. As a Minister, I teach her doctrines; I use her offices; I conform to her rubrics.'

Wesley was a lifelong admirer of the *Book of Common Prayer*, the *Liturgy* and the *Homilies of the Church of England.* He wanted all his people to be regular in their Church attendance, that they might hear and profit from the Liturgy with its use of Scriptures, confession, prayers and collects. All of these are means of grace by which the people of God are built up in their holy faith. Even where the minister was 'unawakened' and often hostile to the revival, Wesley still urged his people to attend the services. He assured them that they would benefit spiritually from hearing the Liturgy read and, especially, partaking in Holy Communion. To that end he instructed his preachers and leaders to make sure that 'Methodist' meeting times did not clash with Church of England services.

As well as advocating regular attendance at the parish church, John Wesley provided additional means of grace for his people. In this way the Methodist 'Class Meeting' was begun. It was made up of eleven people and a leader who met weekly for Bible teaching, testimony, worship and collecting money for the poor.

The 'Band Meeting' was made up of five or six people who were more spiritually advanced and their weekly meeting gave a large place to confession of personal sin and failure and very open and frank discussion. The 'Love Feast' was an occasional meeting for singing, testimony and fellowship together in sharing a simple meal of bread and water. There were also Quarterly Meetings, Watch-night Services and Covenant Services. All these Methodist institutions were for the purpose of helping people to 'grow in grace and in the knowledge of our Lord and Saviour Jesus Christ' (2 Peter 3:18). Just as surely as John Wesley believed in preaching the gospel to bring sinners to saving faith in Christ, he believed just as passionately in encouraging believers to partake of the means of grace. The Christian life, he taught, is not just the experience of a moment of conversion; it is also the spiritual pilgrimage of a lifetime.

15. John Wesley: All The Trumpets Sounded For Him

Throughout his life, we have been looking at different aspects of his life and work and the Methodist Revival of the 18th century.

Wesley is often quoted as saying, 'Our people die well,' and so it is fitting that this final look at the man and his work should be a summary of how he ended his earthly pilgrimage. In November 1753, thinking he was dying, he wrote his own epitaph and described himself as 'a brand plucked from the burning,' a reference both to his dramatic escape from the fire that destroyed his rectory home in 1709, and his escape, through grace, from the fires of damnation. Then in 1783 he was struck down with a serious illness in Bristol and his friends were certain he would not recover. Wesley himself thought likewise and said to Joseph Bradford, his travelling companion, 'I have been reflecting on my past life. I have been wandering up and down between fifty and sixty years, endeavouring in my poor way to do a little good to my fellow creatures. Now it is probable that there are but a few steps between me and death, and what have I to trust to for salvation? I can see nothing which I have done or suffered that will bear looking at. I have no other plea than this:
> I the chief of sinners am
> But Jesus died for me.

But his life was spared for another eight years. On Thursday October 7th, 1790, at the age of 87, he preached his last open-air sermon under an ash tree in Winchelsea in Sussex. Four months later he preached his very last sermon at Leatherhead in Surrey and chose for his text, 'Seek the Lord while He may be found' (Is. 55:6). It marked the end of a remarkable ministry, one unparalleled in the history of the Church. Fifty three years earlier his heart had been 'strangely warmed' in the meeting in Aldersgate Street in London and from that place, his Spirit-anointed ministry had not ceased for more than half a century. On horseback he travelled the roads of Great Britain, covering about a third of a million miles. He had preached more than forty-five times and his 'Methodist' people, in Britain and America, numbered one hundred thousand. He was supported by 300 full-time travelling preachers.

With his brother Charles he had written, edited and published 400 titles including biblical commentaries, letters, sermons, theological treatises, and much else for the edification and of his people. In the final decade of his life he had become one of the best-known men in England and received more invitations to preach than he could possibly accept. Then, in his house in City Road, London, on Sunday, February 26th 1791, he began to enter 'the valley of the shadow of death.' When his friends, knowing his end was near, prayed with him, he replied with a hearty 'Amen.' Then he said to them: 'There is no need for more than what I said at Bristol, "I the chief of sinners am, But Jesus died for me."' Later he said to those gathered round his bed, 'The best of all is, God is with us.' Two days later, as he attempted to repeat the words of Isaac Watts' hymn, 'I'll praise my Maker while I've breath,' his spirit crossed the river, and in Bunyan's immortal words, 'all the trumpets sounded for him on the other side.' In death, as in life, John Wesley proved that saving faith in Christ as Saviour and Lord is the guarantee, the only guarantee, of life eternal.

16. Father, Thy Mercy Never Dies!

The Bible is rich in passages telling us about the mercies of God. The word 'mercy' is wide and comprehensive in meaning, and God's 'mercies' are his 'goodness,' 'love,' 'kindness,' 'favour' and 'grace.' In both the Old and New Testaments God's mercies are spoken of as 'great' (2 Sam. 24:14); 'manifold' (Neh. 9:19); 'tender' (Ps. 25:6); 'endure for ever' (2 Chron. 7:3), 'never come to an end' (Lamentations 3:22); and by them 'we are saved' (Tit.3:5).

Christian biography is full of illustrations of how the people of God in every age have rejoiced as they have found and proved God's mercies in their own lives. One such moving illustration comes from the life and ministry of the Rev. Dr Samuel Parkes Cadman (1864-1936). Between the years 1900 and 1930 Dr Cadman was one of the best-known evangelical preachers in America. For many years he was the minister of the very influential Central Congregational Church in Brooklyn, New York. In his own pulpit and wherever he preached crowds gathered to hear him. Then he began a ministry that gave him even greater fame and popularity as a preacher. He became America's first radio preacher. He was the pioneer of this new means of communicating the gospel to millions of homes. In the 1920s and 30s, Cadman's was the most-recognised voice in every state in the nation. In fact he was so popular that the millions of people who listened to him thought he was an American.

Cadman, however, was born in Shropshire in England, into a very devout Primitive Methodist home. His father, a miner, was a local preacher and class leader. Samuel also became a miner and a local preacher. Later he trained for the ministry in London and then emigrated to America in 1890. As a preacher he was soon a rising star in the Congregational denomination and it was no surprise when he was called to preach in a prestigious pulpit in Brooklyn, New York. Throughout his long ministry Dr Cadman never forgot the Christian teaching and example he had while growing up in a Primitive Methodist home. He often told a true story of an event in his home that made an unforgettable impression upon him. He was nine years old at the time and the incident, so full of spiritual power, stayed with him for the rest of his life.

He came home from school one day to discover that his younger sister had died suddenly and without warning. The whole family was engulfed in grief. His little sister was five years old and was the joy and delight of the family. Now she was gone and the house seemed so silent and lonely without her.

That evening his father was due to take his weekly Class Meeting. He didn't want to leave his family but at the same time he didn't want to disappoint the people waiting for him in the Methodist chapel. After much heart-searching he decided to keep the engagement and he took Samuel with him to the service. Samuel recalled later how he remembered so clearly seeing his father struggling with his emotions. Was it right to go to the chapel? Should he not stay with his broken-hearted wife?

But finally he picked up his hat and coat and Bible and set out to walk to the Class Meeting. He said very little to Samuel as they walked but when they were about half way to the chapel, he stopped. Samuel could see that his father was having a battle with his feelings and he expected him to turn round and go back home. But he didn't. Instead, Cadman recalled, his father did something that was the greatest expression of faith and trust he had ever seen. He stood on the road, took off his hat – and began to sing! In that hour when his heart was breaking with grief and loss and pain, he expressed his deep and unshaken faith in the words of a favourite hymn. He chose the Moravian hymn, first written in German and translated by John Wesley, and so familiar and beloved with all the Methodist people. It begins:

> Now I have found the ground wherein
> Sure my soul's anchor may remain
> The wounds of Jesus for my sin
> Before the world's foundation slain.

'But,' said Dr Cadman, 'it was the fifth verse my father chose to sing that night on the road to the chapel, and I've never forgotten the impression it made on me. With his voice quivering and tears running down his cheeks, he sang his faith in God's unfailing mercies in those wonderful words.'

> Though waves and storms go o'er my head
> Though strength, and health, and friends be gone
> Though joys be withered all and dead
> Though every comfort be withdrawn.
> On this my steadfast soul relies
> Father, Thy mercy never dies!

Father, Thy mercy never dies! Samuel Cadman's father was a devout, Spirit-filled Christian and in his darkest hour he found strength in the sure mercies of God. The love and mercy of God are an ocean that has no bounds. God's amazing love surrounds us in every circumstance of life. When the worst of life's calamities and heartbreaks crowd in upon us and our world seems to be falling apart, His mercies never die! He loves us with an everlasting love (Jer. 31:3).

As the Psalmist discovered the Lord's goodness and mercy follows us all the days of our lives (Ps. 23:6). Our faith and hope and trust are in the love and mercy of the God and Father of our Lord Jesus Christ. Such a faith will hold us, and assure us, and strengthen us, and comfort us, in the darkest hours. Today, tomorrow and every tomorrow what Dr Cadman's father sang about so certainly in his hour of grief is still true – Father, Thy mercy never dies!

17. John Wesley's Doctrines Of The Faith

John Wesley (1703-1791) was the leader of the spiritual movement in 18th century Britain, known as the Methodist movement.

He went to Charterhouse School in London and to Christ Church, Oxford University. There, with his brother Charles (1707–1788), he became the leader of the religious movement. Following two years of ministry in America, he returned to England and had his 'heart strangely warmed' on the 24th May. Preaching to a group of miners in Bristol, his ministry widened and for the next forty eight years, he was engaged in evangelism. What did Wesley believe and preach during those forty eight years?

He began with the love of God. Of all the doctrines found in Wesley's writings, the love of God is prominent. He believed passionately that the God of the Bible, the creator of the world, is a God of love. Certainly Wesley believed that all men and women are sinful but Christ died for us. For fifty years he preached the love of God. All men and women everywhere can be saved, because God loved them and Christ died for them. Wherever in the world we live, regardless of the colour of our skin, the language we speak or our social status, God loved us in his Son.

Secondly, he preached salvation by faith. This is the good news of the gospel. The Spirit enables us to turn away from sin and believe in Jesus. Of the thousands of sermons preached, two of his favourite texts were, 'Believe in the Lord Jesus Christ and you shall be saved' (Ac.16:31), and, 'By grace are you saved through faith' (Eph. 2:8). In a letter to his brother Charles he wrote: 'You and I have nothing to do but save souls.'

Thirdly, he preached the doctrine of the witness of the Spirit. He meant that it is a privilege of every born again believer that his sins are forgiven. The scripture he most often used was Romans 8. 'The same Spirit bears witness with our spirits that we are the children of God' (v.16). The Christian loves God and his neighbour and begins to live the life that manifests the fruit of the Spirit. Wesley knew that this doctrine of the witness of the Spirit brings great joy, peace and assurance to the Christian's heart. This doctrine is found in many of Charles Wesley's hymns. A good example of this is found in the hymn, 'Arise, my soul, arise.' Two lines in one of the stanzas assures us:

> His Spirit answers to the blood
> And tells me I am born of God.

Of course John Wesley's theology contained more than three doctrines. He had a doctrine of creation, a doctrine of the Church, a doctrine of last things, etc. But these three, on the love of God, justification by faith and the witness of the Spirit, were what he called 'the grand fundamental doctrines of Christianity.'

18. My Sons In The Gospel

In the 18th century Evangelical Revival, the names of John Wesley, George Whitefield and Charles Wesley were prominent. These preachers travelled across the country, preaching mostly out-of-doors and attracted large crowds of listeners. In the last two centuries, many biographers, historians and theologians have reminded us of the importance of these preachers. In the days of the Revival Whitefield and the Wesley brothers were mostly ignored by England's parish clergy but there were some notable exceptions. Ministers in the Church of England like George Walker in Truro, David Simpson in Macclesfield, John Fletcher in Madeley, William Grimshaw in Haworth, Henry Crook in Leeds and John Berridge in Everton (Notts.), warmly welcomed the 'Methodist' evangelists into their pulpits. Their support for the revival meant that often they were branded 'Methodists' themselves.

In addition, however, to these clerical supporters, John Wesley had other helpers, some three hundred of them. These were his itinerant preachers, devoted laymen who served as Wesley's lieutenants in circuits all over the British Isles. Many of them were converts of the Wesleys' preaching and John Wesley selected them as full-time itinerants because of their devotion, their passion for evangelism and their willingness to serve under Wesley's directions. He called these good men his 'sons in the gospel' and they served in God's work with great dedication and often at great sacrifice. Many of them had to leave home for months on end as they were appointed to circuits all over the country and there were no resources for married preachers to take their wives and children with them. They were given a horse and saddlebags and little else.

One of the most remarkable of these itinerant preachers was John Nelson, a stonemason from Birstall in Yorkshire. Having gone to London in search of work he was attracted one day to a large gathering of people. Going nearer he discovered that it was a religious meeting and as he listened to John Wesley, without knowing who he was, he came under deep conviction of sin. Nelson felt that Wesley's whole sermon was directed at him and he recorded, 'This man can tell the secrets of my heart, he hath not left me there, for he hath showed me the remedy, even the blood of Jesus.' Following his conversion, Nelson felt called of God to begin to witness to his friends about their salvation. He returned to Birstall and many of his neighbours were converted through his ministry. The stonemason had become a Kingdom builder! He invited John Wesley to Yorkshire who was amazed when he saw the effects of Nelson's preaching. 'The whole town wore a new face. Such a change did God work by the artless testimony of one plain man.' Nelson joined the ranks of Wesley's 'sons in the gospel' and gave the rest of his life to itinerant evangelism. It was Nelson who made contact with Digory and Elizabeth Isbell in Trewint, Cornwall and that contact led to their conversion. He was stationed in Ireland and in every circuit his ministry resulted in conversions. John Nelson was a shining example that the Lord can use lay ministry to His glory as well as that of the ordained clergy.

19. The Reality Of Faith In God

As we enter this new year of 2020 even the most devoted Christians can't ignore the uncertainties we face. Established banking and financial institutions closed down, some of them overnight, and many people feared that not only their life savings but their present jobs were in real danger. Almost daily the news has been gloomy and foreboding and economic experts have been telling us that the situation is the worst in living memory. How do we, as Christians, react to all this? Where do we look? What do we trust in? Has God something to say to us in these days?

I believe He has and it comes to us from a most familiar passage in the Bible – Psalm 23. By any measurement Psalm 23 is one of the best known and loved and repeated chapters in the whole Bible. How we love those familiar words. 'The Lord is my shepherd …He restores my soul ..He leads me …I will dwell in the house of the Lord for ever.' But in the middle of this lovely psalm there are three reminders that Christians are not exempt from the realities of life. The psalmist speaks of 'the paths of righteousness', 'the valley of the shadow' and 'the presence of my enemies.' The mention of 'the paths of righteousness' is a reminder that we are called to love the Lord and live our lives in *righteousness*. The wonderful promises in this psalm come with a condition; they are given to those who determine by God's grace to live righteously. And that must be our first resolution for 2020. The 'valley of the shadow' may refer to death but generally the reference here is wider. It means all those occasions when fear and sorrow and heart-break and loss come to even the best Christians. Then there are our 'enemies.' Originally that probably meant those wanting to kill the psalmist. For us it may be the seduction of old temptations, the fears that paralyse us and the memories of sins that still haunt us.

The psalmist is a realist! As Christians we live our lives in the real world! We are not floating on cloud nine; we are rooted in a fallen world and surrounded by temptations and sins and infirmities. Any day, pain, an incurable disease, even death itself, may come to us or to those we love. How do we face these realities! Psalm 23 has the answer! If we, by God's grace, will walk in 'the paths of righteousness,' then all the promises are ours! The Lord will be our Shepherd. He will lead us by the still waters; He will restore our souls, prepare a table for us in the wilderness, protect and guide us with His rod and staff and, at the end, bring us into the house of the Lord for ever. Let's make Psalm 23 our charter of faith for 2020!

20. More Than Conquerors

In John's Gospel and the Book of the Revelation, Jesus is often spoken of as the Lamb of God. John the Baptist hailed Jesus as 'the Lamb of God who takes away the sin of the world' (John 1:29). In Revelation 5 the myriads of heaven worship him with their song, 'Worthy is the Lamb that was slain' (v.12). Earlier in the chapter he is described as the Lamb standing before the throne and the elders (v.6). Then John adds something very significant; 'as though it had been slain.' Before the throne of Almighty God in heaven stands, not a Lion, but a Lamb; a Lamb still bearing the scars of suffering and death. In these six words John reminds us of the cost of our salvation. The Lamb was slain for the sins of the world. This is victory through sacrifice. Now exalted to the eternal throne, Jesus, the Lamb of God, still bears the scars of sacrifice.

In the Bible we read of scars that symbolise spiritual victory. When Jacob wrestled with the Angel of God by the brook Jabbok, his encounter with God brought spiritual healing. 'Your name will be no more Jacob but Israel' (Gen. 32:28). The old 'Jacob' had become the new 'Israel.' But the cost was a permanent scar as his hip joint was dislocated. The next morning he 'limped' as he passed Penuel (v.31). For the rest of his life the scar would remind him of the event that made him 'Israel,' meaning 'prince with God.' In the New Testament Paul spoke of what it cost him to follow Jesus Christ. 'I bear on my body the scars of Jesus' (Gal. 6:17). Like his Lord, who carried His scars to heaven, Paul's scars bore witness to his faithful ministry.

What about us? Do we have any scars? Has it cost us anything to be loyal to Jesus? Are there marks on our lives that our discipleship has been costly? In warfare the scars received in battle are proudly shown as badges of loyalty. When King Henry V of England addressed his soldiers at Agincourt on the eve of St Crispin's Day, October 24th, 1415, he knew his army was heavily outnumbered. For that momentous occasion Shakespeare put on Henry's lips arguably the greatest speech he ever penned. Every man who fights for Henry will be his brother. And the victory of the field of Agincourt will never be forgotten in England.

> He that shall live this day and see old age
> Will yearly on the vigil feast his neighbours
> And say, 'Tomorrow is St Crispian.'
> Then will he strip his sleeve and show his scars
> And say, 'These wounds I had on Crispian's day.'

'Strip his sleeve and show his scars.' But there's another conflict and the faithful followers of Jesus can expect to have scars. Amy Wilson Carmichael (1867-1951), intrepid Christian missionary in India, wrote about these scars in some very unforgettable and haunting lines.

> Hast thou no scar?
> No hidden scar on foot, or side, or hand?
> I hear thee sung as mighty in the land
> I hear them hail thy bright ascendant star.
> Hast thou no scar
> Hast thou no wound?
> Yet I was wounded by the archers, spent,
> Leaned me against the tree to die, and rent
> By ravening beasts that
> Compassed me, I swooned;
> Hast thou no wound?
> No wound, no scar?
> Yet, as the Master shall the servant be.
> And, pierced are the feet that follow me.
> But thine are whole; can he have followed far
> Who has no wound or scar?

21. Linked Up To The Power

Fifty days on from Easter Sunday the Church celebrates Pentecost. It marks the coming of the Holy Spirit on the disciples and believers who were gathered in an upper room in Jerusalem. The event is recorded in Acts 2 and it tells of the Spirit coming with dramatic signs; a sound like a rushing wind, the appearance of flames of fire and the ability given to the apostles to preach the Good News in languages they had not learned. When Jesus had earlier spoken to his disciples about the coming of the Spirit, he emphasised spiritual power. 'You will receive power when the Holy Spirit comes upon you' (Acts 1:8). And that promise was marvellously fulfilled. When the Spirit came on that Pentecost morning, the apostles began to witness boldly. They preached salvation in the name of the risen and ascended Lord Jesus (Acts 2:37-42). On that day some three thousand men and women believed in Jesus as Lord and Messiah and were baptised (v.41). Later it is recorded that the apostles gave testimony to Christ's resurrection 'with great power' (Acts 4:33). All through the book of Acts we see the Christian Church preaching and witnessing, suffering and serving with great spiritual power. Even their enemies spoke of them as 'turning the world upside down' (Acts 17:6).

At this Pentecost season we need to recapture the power of the Spirit. Perhaps our lack of power is because something has gone wrong with our spiritual connections. Maybe we are not 'linked up' to the Spirit as those early Christians were. I recall an event of many years ago that illustrates the importance of being 'linked up.' I had returned home from college during the summer holidays to the farm in Northern Ireland where I had grown up. Some months earlier electrical power had come to that part of the country for the first time. One evening in late August, I visited one of our neighbours. His farm lay next to ours and I was talking with him in one of his fields. Across his farm and ours there had been installed a line of wooden poles. These poles supported the electric cables. We were standing near one of these poles and it carried a notice stamped into an aluminum plate. It warned that some 33,000 volts of electric power were running through the wires.

As we stood there that summer evening, we could hear the current humming in the wires. An hour later I was in my neighbour's home – and it was lit with oil lamps! He had 33,000 volts of electric power passing over his farm but he had none in his house. He was not 'linked up' to the supply.

Often in the Church we are like that. We have the services, the programmes, the plans, the personnel – but not the power of the Spirit that convicts sinners and brings them to faith in Jesus. There is little danger that we will turn even the parish upside down, much less the world! This Pentecost celebration is a time to get 'linked up' to the Holy Spirit.

22. Suddenly My Mind Felt Clothed With Light

Elizabeth Gurney was born into a family of devout Quakers in Norwich. Her father was a successful factory owner and a partner in the Gurney Bank. Her mother, Catherine Gurney, was a member of the famous Barclay banking family. It was a sermon that brought Elizabeth to the place of personal faith and commitment to God. She had gone to hear an American Quaker, William Savery, preach in Norwich, and she asked her father to invite him home to dinner. The effect of Savery's sermon and his conversation with Elizabeth changed her life. Later she wrote, 'I think my feelings that night were the most exalted I remember. Suddenly my mind felt clothed with light, as with a garment, and I felt silenced before God. I cried with the heavenly feeling of humility and repentance.' Every Christian's 'Damascus Road' is special to them. Elizabeth Gurney recorded her conversion in the language common among Quakers, speaking about the coming of 'the light' and feeling 'silenced' before God.

The immediate results of Elizabeth's conversion were her deep desires to help those in need. She collected clothes from her well-to-do friends and relations and gave them to the poor. She began a systematic visitation of the sick and organised a Sunday School in her home where she taught the children to read. At the age of 20 she married Joseph Fry, the son of a very successful banker and also a Quaker. They set up home in east London and Elizabeth's ministry to the poor continued. She became a preacher among the Quakers and in 1811 she attended the meeting that set up the British and Foreign Bible Society, the fore-runner of today's Bible Society.

When a friend invited her to visit the women prisoners in Newgate Prison in London, Elizabeth was appalled at what she found. The over-crowding and lack of hygiene facilities made the conditions deplorable and Elizabeth Fry began a campaign of social, moral and religious improvement for the inmates. She gave evidence in the House of Commons about London prisons, spoke against the death penalty, and used every possible means to bring about prison reforms. Queen

Victoria admired Elizabeth's work, met her on a number of occasions and gave money to promote her enterprises. When she died in October 1845, the great work she had begun continued and her name will always be remembered in connection with her concern for the poor and especially for women prisoners. Elizabeth Fry's conversion was much more than a personal conversion; it set her on the road not only to love God but also to love her neighbour.

23. Praying In The Silence Of The Heart

'O Lord of hosts … if you will give me a son …I will give him to the Lord all the days of his life' (1 Sam 1:11). Three 'C's will help us to grasp this most personal and moving prayer. First, the prayer's context. Hannah was the childless wife of Elkanah, who had sons and daughters by his other wife, Peninnah. As she longed for a child, she was taunted by 'her rival' (v.6) who reproached her for being barren. It doesn't take much imagination to understand how miserable and lonely and useless Hannah felt. Although Elkanah loved Hannah, his well-meant sympathy, 'Am I not more to you than ten sons?' (v.8) was hardly calculated to ease her pain! Making the annual pilgrimage to the Tabernacle at Shiloh, Hannah was 'deeply distressed, prayed to the Lord and wept bitterly' (v.10). This is the Bible's first record of a woman praying. We can be certain that godly women, long before Hannah's time, had prayed but this is the first mention in Scripture of a woman praying.

Secondly, the prayer's content. Above everything else, Hannah longed to have a son. 'O Lord of hosts, if you will look on my affliction and give me a son, I will give him back to you in service all the days of his life' (v.11). It was a cry from the heart. A lonely wife, longing for a child, taunted by her rival, and not really understood by her husband, poured out her very soul in grief. And it was all done without spoken words! As her lips moved, Eli the priest, misreading the signs, rebuked her for being drunk (v.14). There are times when the burden of our heart is so great that no words can express it, but how comforting to know that God hears us!

Thirdly, the prayer's consequences. The Lord graciously answered Hannah's distress and a year later she was nursing her baby son! (vv. 21,22). Hannah's dark night had been eclipsed by a glorious morning. Grief and sorrow had given way to joy and delight but as she cradled her infant son, Hannah did not forget what she had promised the Lord. In token of His faithfulness, she named her son Samuel, meaning, 'asked of the Lord' (v.20). Some time later Hannah took Samuel to

Shiloh and presented him to Eli, fulfilling the promise she had made to the Lord. Hannah's dedication of Samuel is a reminder to all of us not only to give thanks to God for answered prayer but also to carry out whatever vows or promises we've made to Him. Hannah's words to Eli are so full of praise and gratitude to God that they need no comment. Let them inspire thanksgiving in our hearts. 'For this child I prayed …therefore as long as he lives he is lent to the Lord' (v.28).

24. A Child Shall Lead Them

Down the centuries since Old Testament times many Jewish and Christian parents have named a baby son Samuel. They have been attracted by the story of the baby who was so longed for, who was given to the Lord at his birth and who grew up a man of God and a judge and prophet in Israel. The story of Samuel's birth is told with great pathos in the opening chapter of the first book of Samuel. We are introduced to Elkanah who had two wives. One wife, Peninnah, bore him children but his other wife, Hannah, was childless. Hardly surprisingly the situation made for great tension in the home and Hannah was broken-hearted and desperate for a child. Her misery was made worse when Peninnah 'provoked her' so much that she wept bitterly and would not eat. And Elkanah's response lacked feeling to say the least. 'Why are you grieving?' he asked Hannah, 'am I not better to you than ten sons?' On the yearly pilgrimage at Shiloh, Hannah poured out her heart to God, praying she would have a son. Even when the priest Eli mistook her silent prayers for drunken ramblings she refused to give up and promised the Lord that is she had a son, he would be dedicated to God for his whole life.

We can only imagine Hannah's joy when she gave birth to a baby boy the following year. And she knew exactly what has name should be – Samuel, meaning 'asked of God.' After Samuel was weaned he was taken to the Tabernacle in Shiloh so that, in Hannah's words, he should be 'loaned to the Lord as long as he lives' (1 Sam. 1:28). There in Shiloh Samuel was called of God in a vision to be a leader in Israel and until his death, he was both judge and prophet to his people. As an old man he anointed Saul as Israel's first king and later he anointed David. When he died the historian records that 'all Israel mourned for him' (28:3). The baby who was prayed for and who was dedicated to God grew up to be a spiritual leader to his people. As Christian parents we pray and hope and believe that our children will follow the Lord. Samuel's story reminds us that our part is to surround our children with love and care and prayer and dedication.

25. The Prayer From The Depth Of Despair

Jonah 2:2-9. Twice in the Bible there is a record of prayers prayed in hell. In Jesus' parable of the Rich Man and Lazarus, the former prayed for both release from his torment and that a warning would be sent to his family (Luke 16:24-31). Here in the book of Jonah this chapter opens with the words, 'Then Jonah prayed to the Lord his God' (v.1) The prophet prayed from what he described as 'the belly of hell' (KJV), or 'from the depth of Sheol' (v.2). The first chapter of the book tells how Jonah was commissioned by God to go and preach in Ninevah, the capital city of the great Assyrian Empire. Instead Jonah ran away from his home country, from (he thought) the presence of God and from hearing God's command. The Assyrians had long been the all-conquering enemies of Israel and Jonah was either afraid to go to Ninevah, or he did not want them to hear God's word – or both. So he ran away and took ship for Tarshish (i.e. Spain). During a violent storm he confessed to the sailors that he had disobeyed God and reluctantly they threw him overboard (1:12-14). The Lord had 'appointed a great fish' which swallowed the prophet and from deep inside its belly, he prayed to the Lord. God heard Jonah's prayer, the fish spewed him out and his life was spared (2:10).

Jonah's prayer, prayed when he was sure he was about to die, has much to reach us about praying. *First*, even in our disobedience, God hears us when we pray humbly and sincerely. Jonah's terrible calamity was directly the result of his running away from God. It wasn't because of circumstances, it wasn't inevitable, it wasn't fate or just 'one of those things;' it was his disobedience brought about the disaster. How gracious God is! Even in our running away from Him, He still loves us and hears our prayers. *Second*, we can pray anywhere. If Jonah could cry to the Lord when, in his own words, 'in the heart of the seas,' when 'all the waves and billows' passed over him (v.3), how many places may we not find to come before the Lord in prayer? There is the quiet time at the day's beginning, a moment of reflection in a busy schedule, between meetings, as we drive the car or travel in the bus, or plane or ship – so many places where we can 'lift up our hearts' to the

Lord. *Third*, no situation is too difficult for God. The God who 'hurled a great wind upon the sea' (1:4), who 'appointed a great fish to swallow up Jonah' (1:17); who prepared a 'a plant' and 'a worm' to bring about His purposes (4:6,7), is the Sovereign Lord of earth and heaven. He can hear us and help us in our deepest distress, in the hours when life seems to be tumbling in all round us. *Fourth*, the Lord can deliver! Jonah's prayer from the depth of hell ends with the ringing assurance, 'Deliverance belongs to the Lord' (2:9). We all need to hear that! Today, whatever our need, our pain, our disappointment, our fear, our weakness, our besetting sin - with the Lord there is deliverance.

26 A Flaming Evangelist

Twenty five miles north-east of Huddersfield is the village of Haworth, the setting for the ministry of the Revd William Grimshaw, in many ways the most remarkable and successful of all the Anglican Methodists. Haworth, in Yorkshire, has a large influx of visitors every year and most are drawn by the Bronte connection. As the sightseers wend their way along the narrow street, gaze into the curio shops and wander round the parish church, how few realise the sixty years before the Revd Patrick Bronte came to Haworth, the most illustrious of his predecessors was the enthusiastic and courageous Grimshaw. Yet today you will search Haworth in vain for any reminder of Grimshaw except his name among the lists of incumbents in the church, a memento in the Bronte Museum and an inscription in West Lane Methodist Church.

Grimshaw was born on September 14th, 1708, the same year as Charles Wesley. After studying at Cambridge he was ordained into the Anglican ministry in 1731 and in 1732 he began his work at Haworth. The year 1738 is stamped in Methodist history as the year of the Wesley's awakening and it was no less eventual in Grimshaw's life. Although active in ministry, he had no personal peace with God and in 1738 he entered the first of many covenants with God in his search for grace and assurance. The sudden death of his first wife in 1739 deepened his despair and his renewed covenants and search for peace made his friend, Benjamin Ingham, one of the Oxford Holy Club, say: 'Mr Grimshaw, you are a Jew, you are no believer in Jesus Christ, you are building on the sand.' Light came at last – through the writings of the Puritan John Owen. Reading Owen's 'Justification,' Grimshaw entered into life abundant and found peace of soul. That was in 1742, a watershed in Grimshaw's life and a year to be remembered in the history of British and American revivals. It was a year of revivals and had been preceded by earlier awakenings.

The year 1743 saw the awakening in New England under the preaching of Jonathan Edwards; Howell Harris began his labours in Wales in

1735 and in April 1739, John Wesley took his first stand in the open-air. Scotland also experienced an awaking in 1739 and this work spread rapidly when George Whitefield visited Scotland for the second time in 1742. Grimshaw was destined to play a leading part in the kindling of the fires that burned in the North of England. The first contact between Grimshaw and the Methodists was in October 1746. John Nelson, the stonemason turned kingdom builder, was the most effective of Wesley's lay preachers in the North and had planted Methodism in the West Riding of Yorkshire, particularly in Leeds, Bradford and Birstall. Visiting these societies in 1746, Charles Wesley was invited to meet Grimshaw. It would be an eventful occasion.

Charles Wesley preached in Grimshaw's church and noted in his *Journal*, 'All listened, many wept, some were comforted.' But three months later the rising tide of ecclesiastical opposition to the Wesley's made Grimshaw fearful of allowing a Methodist in his pulpit and Charles Wesley remonstrated with him for his timidity. In May 1747, John Wesley came to Haworth and preached in Grimshaw's church to 'to more than the church could contain.' In a short time, Grimshaw had become John Wesley's 'lieutenant' in the North of England. He was the first parish minister in England to engage in extra-parochial preaching and it brought him plenty of criticism, ecclesiastical rebuke and mob violence. In August 1748 Grimshaw, John Wesley and their assistants were met by a mob at Colne, in Lancashire, as violent as any ever encountered by the itinerants. Wesley was punched in the face, Grimshaw was thrown to the ground and trampled in the mud and another preacher was almost drowned when flung into the river. Grimshaw was as strong and burly as Wesley was small and slight, but both were undaunted. In an official letter Wesley expostulated. 'Proceed against us by the law if you can or dare, but not by lawless violence; nor by making a drunken, cursing, swearing, riotous mob both judge, jury and executioner. This is flat rebellion against God and the King, as you may possibly find to your cost.' But as usual the magistrates took no action and for the next decade, mob violence would be the common experience of the travelling preacher and Grimshaw was not excepted.

To the present day the legend persists that Grimshaw of Haworth was mad. The poet, Robert Southey, thought Grimshaw had been mad but what are the facts? If believing that men without Christ are dying in their sins is madness, then Grimshaw was mad. If preaching destruction against those who 'obey not the Gospel of the Lord Jesus Christ' is thought madness, then certainly Grimshaw was mad. If going out into the highways to win men and women for Christ is considered madness, then the charge is well founded. If the ignoring of ecclesiastical protocol in the interests of men's souls is accepted as proof of madness, then Grimshaw must be pronounced guilty. John Wesley thought highly of 'good Mr Grimshaw' and appointed him in charge of all the Methodist societies in the North of England. In 1751 Wesley drew up an important Deed that declared the Wesleys and Grimshaw to have sole authority in appointing and stationing Methodist preachers. If Grimshaw outlived the Wesleys, the Deed made his the controlling hand on the Methodist societies. Writing to Ebenezer Blackwell in July 1761, John Wesley said of Grimshaw, 'I have been with him for some days, an Israelite indeed. A few such as him would make a nation tremble. He carries fire wherever he goes.'

For 20 years Grimshaw was a familiar figure all over the North. In the mid-18th century, most of that part of England was impassable for wheeled traffic and Grimshaw went everywhere on foot. He seldom followed the roads, such as existed, but crossed the fields, climbed stone walls and hedges and preached twenty five times to thirty times each week. His strong frame, resonant voice and indomitable courage were admirably suited to the bleak Yorkshire moors and the people who inhabited them. Captured brilliantly in Emily Bronte's 'Wuthering Heights,' the people of the moors were at best suspicious of strangers and often openly hostile, but Grimshaw feared neither the face nor fist of any man. In his quest for souls he took the kingdom of heaven by storm and would resort to any stratagem or practical joke to gain the attention of his hearers. Learning that some of the parishioners made the pretence of coming to church on Sunday morning but instead went drinking in the local inn, Grimshaw determined to deal with the offenders. Leaving the congregation to sing a long psalm, he took his bullwhip, went to the inn and literally whipped out any of his parishioners he found there. 'You left home to come to church and to church you shall go.' In church Grimshaw constantly proclaimed: 'If you will be damned, it shall be long of yourselves, for I will be clear of your blood.' On uninvited visits to non-church-goers' homes he would cry out: 'I know that I am not welcome, but I will speak to every one under my care concerning his soul. If you will not hear me, you shall hear me at home; and if you will perish, you will perish with the sound of the gospel in your ears.' Standing today by the door of Grimshaw's church and looking across his parish, it is easy to understand why John Wesley thought so highly of Grimshaw.

Reported to his bishop for allegedly neglecting his own parish, Grimshaw was summoned to Wakefield to answer the charge before Archbishop Hutton. 'Mr Grimshaw, how many communicants did you have at your quarterly sacrament when you first came to Haworth?' 'Twelve, my lord.' 'How many have you now?' 'In the winter,' replied Grimshaw, 'from four to five hundred and in the summer nearly twelve hundred.' The charges were dropped!

Grimshaw was a hell-fire preacher, as John Pawson said to Charles Wesley. 'No other preaching will do in Yorkshire but the old sort, that comes like thunder-claps upon the conscience, for fine preaching doth more harm than good here.' When Whitefield implied that the Haworth parishioners needed no extra spiritual help, having such a minister, Grimshaw protested. 'Oh, sir, for God's sake do not speak so. I pray you do not flatter them. I fear the greater part of them are going to hell with their eyes open.' Grimshaw dealt with every man alike, faithfully and direct. He rebuked Lord Huntingdon to his face when he suspected him of being more interested in theological debate than holy living. 'My lord, if you needed information, I would gladly to my utmost to assist you, but the fault is not in your head but in your heart which can only be reached by a divine power.' Grimshaw died on April 7th, 1763, a truly apostolic man.

Today, of course, Haworth is thought of more in connection with the Revd Patrick Bronte and his famous offspring than of the fiery evangelist who preceded him at his church. Patrick Bronte (1777-1861) was a native of Co Down, Ireland, entered St John's College, Cambridge, and afterwards took Holy Orders and held various curacies until he was appointed in 1820 to the incumbency of Haworth, which he retained until his death forty one years later.

27. What A Friend We Have In Jesus

We can have the friendship of Jesus! Joseph Scriven's hymn, written in 1857, beginning 'What a friend we have in Jesus,' has become one of the most popular of all our commonly sung hymns. It reminds us that the love and mercy of God is always with us in Jesus; he is not only our Saviour and Lord and Redeemer but he is also our Friend. Many people who love this hymn may not know that it was written from deep personal tragedy and that the author had good reason for writing about Jesus as his friend. Joseph Scriven was born near Banbridge in Co Down, Northern Ireland, in 1819. After graduating from Trinity College, Dublin, he was engaged to be married. On the eve of the wedding, his bride-to-be, a keen horse rider, was thrown from her horse while crossing the river Bann and was drowned. Scriven was shattered by the tragedy and some time later emigrated to Canada.

Although his faith was tested to the limit by his fiancé's untimely death, he did not turn away from the Lord or blame Him. When he came to write his famous hymn years later, the memory of the tragedy is reflected in the opening lines.

> What a friend we have in Jesus
> All our sins and griefs to bear
> What a privilege to carry
> Everything to God in prayer.

'All our griefs.' Joseph Scriven wrote from his heart and spoke for so many who have passed the same way. The burden of grief can be such that it blots out everything else and can become unbearable. Scriven, however, had learned, as we can learn, that Jesus our Lord is a true friend, for He has 'borne our griefs and carried our sorrows' (Is.53:4). But Scriven's heartbreak was not over. Some years after settling in Canada, he became engaged to a Christian girl. By now he had joined what was then known as the Plymouth Brethren who strongly emphasised that all adult Christians should be baptised by immersion. His second bride-to-be, Eliza Roche, requested immersion and the elders of the assembly baptised her in the local lake. She caught a chill and died from it later. Scriven was heart-broken again. Twice death caused by water had taken away the woman he loved. The pathos and pain of a twice-broken heart lies behind the lines:

> Have we trials and temptations?
> Is there trouble anywhere?
> We should never be discouraged
> Take it to the Lord in prayer.

After many years absence Scriven returned to his hometown, Banbridge, but not many people knew or remembered him. He found few friends an after some time he went back to Canada. He had written the first two verses of the hymn but now added a third, prompted by the cold welcome he had received.

> Do thy friends despise, forsake thee?
> Take it to the Lord in prayer
> In His arms He'll take and shield thee
> Thou wilt find a solace there.

The sad story of Joseph Scriven's life is not generally known but when we know the facts, it makes this popular hymn even more inspiring. Out of deep hurt and loss and grief and pain, Scriven wrote about the friendship of Jesus. Whatever burdens us today, however painful the circumstances and no matter how dark our night seems to be, this great hymn comes to us with unfailing assurance.

> Precious Saviour, still our refuge
> Take it to the Lord in prayer.

28. John Wesley And The Methodist Pentecost

'Till you press the believers to expect full salvation *now*, you must not look for any revival.' John Wesley wrote these words in 1766 after observing the work of God in the Methodist movement for twenty-five years. He had seen the evidence among the Methodist converts. Whenever Christians longed for heart purity and the blessing of full salvation there was a corresponding 'knock-on' effect in the whole work of God. Holiness and revival were linked; when believers sought entire sanctification the work of evangelism caught fire. Early in 1760 there was a remarkable move of the Spirit among the Methodist people in Otley in West Yorkshire. Although it began in a small way it was a spark that caused a very large conflagration. The revival was so impressive that John Wesley took time to visit Otley and talk with those caught up in a very significant work of the Holy Spirit. He wrote:

> In the beginning of the year 1760 there was a great revival of the work of God in Yorkshire. About 30 persons were met together in Otley in the evening in order as usual to pray, sing hymns, and to provoke one another to love and good works. When they came to speak of the several states of their souls, some with deep sighs and groans complained of the heavy burden from the remains of inbred sin. ...One cried out in an agony, 'Lord, deliver me from my sinful nature,' then a second, a third and a fourth. ...Thus they continued for the space of two hours, some praising and magnifying God, some crying to Him for pardon or purity of heart. Before they parted, three believed God had fulfilled His word and cleansed them from all unrighteousness.'

Years later John Wesley wrote of the Otley revival that it was 'a glorious work of sanctification.' There had been other revivals among the Methodists, like those at Everton in 1759 and in Weardale in 1772, but none of these had been as deep, as far-reaching and as long lasting as the Otley revival. Its effects were felt in most of the English Methodist Societies and also in Ireland. John Wesley referred to it as a day of Pentecost. 'Many years ago my brother frequently said, "Your day of Pentecost is not fully come, but I doubt not it will. And then you will hear of persons

sanctified as frequently as you do now of persons justified."'
Having carefully observed the Otley revival John Wesley was
convinced that Charles' prediction was indeed fulfilled.

The Methodist Pentecost had come! If John Wesley, always exact
and definite in his use of words, likened the work at Otley to that
which launched the Church in Jerusalem, then we can be sure it was
a revival of great spiritual power. When the history of this
Yorkshire move of the Spirit is carefully traced, the undeniable
evidence is that wherever the spiritual flame spread, hundreds were
converted and many believer experienced the blessing of entire
sanctification. The following quotations from John Wesley's
Journals and *Letters* are representative of many more that clearly
prove that, in Wesley's own words, 'the word of God was as a fire
among the stubble.'

> September 21st, 1761. 'Here likewise (at Bristol), I had the
> satisfaction to observe a considerable increase of the work of
> God. The congregations were exceeding large and the people
> hungering and thirsting after righteousness... God was pleased
> to pour out His Spirit this year on every part both of England and
> Ireland.' July 24th, 1762. 'I rode to Dublin and found the flame
> was not only continuing but increasing.' A letter from Limerick
> in the west of Ireland confirmed that 'a glorious work' was going
> on there and 'the fire is now spreading on every side.' Wesley
> returned to England from Ireland to hear that the fires of the Spirit
> were burning in many places. From Cheshire came the news that
> 'there was an outpouring of the Spirit, nor is His hand yet stayed.'
> In Liverpool found 'such a work of God as had never been known
> there before.' At the close of 1762 Wesley reflected. 'I now
> stood and looked back on the past year; a year of uncommon
> trials and uncommon blessings. Abundance have been
> convinced of sin, very many have found peace with God, and in
> London only I believe full two hundred have been brought into
> glorious liberty.'

Eighteen years after the outbreak of the Methodist Pentecost, John
Wesley's judgement on its spiritual impact had not changed. 'The
glorious work of sanctification spread from 1760, first through

various parts of Yorkshire, afterwards in London …Dublin …and all the south and west of Ireland. And wherever the work of sanctification increased, the whole work of God increased in all its branches.' The Otley awakening convinced John Wesley that there is a vital connection between entire sanctification and revival. 'Where Christian perfection is not strongly and clearly enforced, the believers grow dead and cold.' 'Where Christian perfection is little insisted upon, be the preachers ever so eloquent, there is little increase, either in the number or grace of the hearers.'

The Methodist Pentecost that began in Otley in Yorkshire in January 1760 brought great blessing and increase to the Methodist work all over England and Ireland. The Pentecostal blessing that sanctified believers also awakened sinners and brought them to salvation. No wonder Charles Wesley taught the Methodist people to sing.

> See how great a flame aspires
> Kindled by a spark of grace!
> Jesu's love the nations fires
> Sets the kingdoms on a blaze.
> To bring fire on earth He came
> Kindled in some hearts it is
> O that all might catch the flame
> All partake the glorious bliss!

29. The King Had Another Move

Of all the folktales that circulated in Europe in the centuries past none was more widespread or popular than that surrounding Dr Faustus. Supposedly a brilliant German alchemist living in the early 16th century, Faustus began to delve into witchcraft and finally made a pact with the Devil. For 24 years he would have everything he wanted but at the end of that time the Devil would claim his soul.

The story was popularised in England by Christopher Marlowe in 1604, in his *Dr Faustus*, and in Germany, two centuries later, in Johann Goethe's *Faust*. The Devil kept his promise and for twenty-four years Faustus enjoyed fame, knowledge and the satisfaction of every desire. But the years rolled quickly by and Faustus was gripped with terrible foreboding as the end drew near. On his last night he met a fearful death as the Devil claimed his soul for damnation. The drama attracted an artist who committed it to canvas. He depicted Faustus and the Devil playing chess and he entitled it 'Checkmate.' The game is over and the Devil has won. He gloats across the chess table at the doomed Faustus whose face is rigid with terror. The picture hung in a French gallery and many people came to see it. One day a great master of the game came to view it. He gazed at it intently for hour after hour. Suddenly the silence was broken by his cry, 'It's a lie! The game is not over! The king has another move!' The chess master saw what everyone else had missed. In the picture Faustus still has his king. The king can yet bring victory out of seeming disaster.

On the first Easter, the enemies of Jesus were jubilant. The chief priests, the scribes and the Pharisees, had all conspired to put him to death. How they hated Him! He had done mighty works. He had healed the sick; he had cast out demons from the tormented; he had calmed the storms and raised the dead. But they rejected Him, branded Him a blasphemer and brought about his arrest, trial and execution. The Romans, thinking Him just another rabble-rousing nationalist, were glad to see him dead. So the Jews and the Romans celebrated while the body of Jesus lay on the cold slab in Joseph's grave. They had triumphed! He was gone! He was dead! He was buried! He would not come back! His followers were scattered. He would soon be forgotten. The brief story of Jesus of Nazareth had ended in the tomb.

But they were all wrong! wrong!! wrong!!! The game was not over! The king had another move! The King of Heaven raised His Son Jesus from death, never to die again (Rom. 6:9). And Christians have been celebrating that great event for two thousand years! But there's more! In all our lives, in every difficulty, in every need, in every heartbreak, in all of life's darkest hours – our King is with us. And He always has another move!

30. John Wesley – Man Of One Book

Near the end of his life, John Wesley wrote of how he had loved and believed the Scriptures from his earliest days. 'From a child I was taught to love and reverence the Scripture, the oracles of God.' This devotion to Scripture as the Word of God characterised Wesley's entire life and ministry. He described how 'Methodism' began at Oxford University in the late 1720s.

'Four young men united together, each of them was *homo unius libri* – a man of one book. God taught them all to make his 'Word a lantern unto their feet, and a light in all their paths.' They had one, and only one rule of judgment with regard to all their tempers, words, and actions, namely, the oracles of God. They were one and all determined to be *Bible-Christians*. They were continually reproached for this very thing; some terming them in derision *Bible-bigots*; others *Bible-moths* – feeding, they said, upon the Bible as moths do upon cloth. And indeed unto this day it is their constant endeavour to think and speak as the oracles of God.'

The phrase *homo unius libri*, meaning 'man of one book,' became a description of how John Wesley made Scripture the foundation for both his faith and his practice. He didn't mean by it that he read only the Bible. Far from it. The evidence from his *Journal* and his *Letters* tells us that he was one of the most widely read men of his century in England. From his days at Oxford University and throughout his busy life, he read widely in philosophy, history, biography, poetry, medicine and travel as well as divinity, theology and Church history. By 'man of one book' he meant that all other books were compared to the ONE book – the Bible. When he published the first series of his sermons in 1746, he described his own method of reading and studying the Bible.

> Here then, I am, far from the busy ways of men. I sit down alone: only God is here. In his presence I open, I read his Book; for this end, to find the way to heaven. Is there a doubt concerning the meaning of what I read? Does anything appear dark or intricate? I lift up my heart to the Father of lights: 'Lord, is it not thy Word, "If any man lack wisdom, let him ask of God?"… Thou hast said,

"If any man be willing to do thy will, he shall know." I am willing to do, let me know thy will.'

Almost the first thing we notice when we read any of John Wesley's publications is how often he quoted and made references to Scripture. This is not only true of his sermons but of all his other publications as well. They are all punctuated with quotations from the Biblical books. Wesley knew the Biblical text so well that he was able to weave the very words of Scripture into all his writings. He encouraged all his 'Methodist' people to read and study the Scriptures diligently and he advised them in particular to pray for the Holy Spirit's help in understanding what the Scriptures mean.

To help them further he published his *Explanatory Notes Upon The New Testament* in 1755 and his *Explanatory Notes Upon The Old Testament* in 1765. These *Notes* were brief but helpful explanations of what the Biblical text means. The 'man of one book' wanted all those under his pastoral care to love and cherish and study the Scriptures as he did. He insisted that Scripture not only gives us information but that it also gives us counsel, direction and warning. We must not only read the Bible and study it and believe it – we must obey it! The Scriptures alone show us the way of salvation. When he taught and emphasised the Biblical doctrine of sanctification he constantly referred to it as Scriptural holiness. Explaining his 'Methodist' ministry to the Revd Henry Venn in Huddersfield in 1763, he wrote of himself, tongue in cheek, 'If I am a heretic, I became such by reading the Bible.'

Always practical in his counsels to his people, he directed them to read and study the Bible regularly every morning and evening. His advice, given two and half centuries ago, is still good counsel for us as we live our busy lives in the 21st century.

> If you desire to read the Scriptures in such a manner as may most effectually answer this end (to understand the things of God), would it not be advisable (1) to set apart a little time, if you can, every morning and evening for this purpose? (2) At each time, if you have leisure, to read a chapter out of the Old, and one out of

the New Testament; if you cannot do this, to take a single chapter, or a part of one? (3) To read this with a single eye to know the whole will of God, and a fixed resolution to do the same.

31. Justin: Who Was The Man?

Sometime in the summer of 165AD seven Christian men were put to death in Rome. Accused of belonging to an illicit religion, they refused point blank to offer sacrifices to pagan gods. Threatened with torture and execution they replied that suffering and death gave them confidence to appear at the Great Tribunal 'of our Lord and Saviour.' The sentence was pronounced and having been scourged, all seven were beheaded. Their leader was named Justin and we know him in Church History as Justin the Martyr. His conversion to Christianity, although a quiet and low key affair, is a story that should be known.

Justin was born in the year 100AD in Samaria, near the modern town of Nablus. His family was Gentile and pagan and as a young man Justin was drawn to the study of philosophy. Soon he was a recognised pagan philosopher and he began to travel as an itinerant teacher, wearing the distinctive cloak of the philosophers. He tells us that his search for truth led him to study the various schools of Greek philosophy but in none of them could he find the assurance he was looking for. Then something happened that radically changed his life. Walking one evening on a sea shore, he fell into conversation with an old man. Justin listened as the old man told him that the prophecies of the Hebrew Bible had been fulfilled and they could be found in the writings of the Christian Bible. He further told Justin that truth can only be known through the one true God and that His Spirit would enlighten Justin. Justin was deeply moved by the conversation, began to read the New Testament – and was converted to faith in Christ.

Now a Christian believer Justin continued to travel, still wearing his philosopher's cloak but now preaching and teaching the Christian gospel. He wrote two *Apologies* explaining and defending the Christian faith. He travelled to Asia Minor and finally to Rome where he taught in a Christian school. His strong defence of Christianity came to the notice of the authorities and he was arrested with six of his friends. Refusing to acknowledge pagan gods, they were executed together. Who was the old man who introduced Justin to Christianity?

We don't know and Justin doesn't even tell us his name, if he knew it. Justin's conversion happened because a Christian witnessed to him. We should use every opportunity we have to pass on the Good News!

.

32. Pilgrim Places

The Christian Church was born in the city of Jerusalem in the great events of our Lord's death and resurrection and the coming of the Holy Spirit at Pentecost. It spread rapidly across the Roman world and other cities became important Christian centres. These included Antioch, Ephesus, Alexandria, Constantinople and Rome. At the beginning of the 6th century a small town in southeast England was added to that illustrious list – Canterbury in Kent. It seemed more likely that London or Winchester or Lincoln would have become the centre of English Christianity but a missionary's decision to make Canterbury his headquarters gave the honour to a town formerly fairly insignificant. That missionary was Augustine (died 604/605AD), a Benedictine monk from a monastery in Rome and not to be confused with the much better known Bishop Augustine of Hippo in North Africa (354-430).

Augustine was selected for this mission to England by Bishop Gregory of Rome. We are not sure why Gregory initiated this mission but there is a well-known story about it. This story, or legend, is told in the Venerable Bede's great work on English Church History, *Ecclesiastical History of the English People*. Bede tells us that while Bishop Gregory was visiting the Forum in Rome, he saw children for sale in the slave market. Noting their fair complexions and blue eyes, he asked who they were and was told they were Angles, captured in their home country, England. Tradition says that Gregory replied with a Latin pun. *'Non Angli, sed angeli,'* 'not Angles but angels.' Another tradition, however, says that the visitors to the Forum were merchants, not slave children. Whatever the truth of the incident, Gregory sent Augustine and forty other monks on a mission to England to convert the native peoples to Christianity.

Of course this was not the first time the Christian faith reached Britain. The gospel had come to these islands at least three hundred years before Augustine's mission. Who brought the Good News to our ancestors is uncertain. It might have come with Roman soldiers or traders, for the Romans had occupied the country as early as 43AD. More likely, however, it was Christian missionaries from Gaul (France), our nearest neighbours across the English Channel, who first evangelised our pagan forefathers. When an important Church Council was held in Arles in France in 314AD, the records show that three English bishops attended, indicating that early in the 4th century Christianity was well enough established in England to have at least three bishoprics.

Augustine landed in Kent in 597AD and made his headquarters at Canterbury. Ethelbert, King of Kent, had married Bertha, a Frankish Christian, and although he was not a Christian, he allowed Bertha to practise her faith. She had brought her chaplain, Bishop Liudhard, with her and they worshipped at an old Christian site in Canterbury. There is good reason to believe that this is the very place where St Martin's Church stands today, almost certainly named after Martin of Tours (died 397AD), the former soldier turned monk who evangelised Gaul. If this is indeed the site where Queen Bertha and later her husband Ethelbert worshipped, then what a Christian heritage is here. Just think of it! In this year of grace 2008 we can stand by St Martin's Church and know that, without a break, Trinitarian worship has been offered on this site for at least 1400 years! That makes St Martin's the oldest place of continuous worship in the land.

From Canterbury Augustine and his monks began their evangelism and in a short time King Ethelbert professed the Christian faith and was baptised. Ethelbert's kingdom stretched as far north as the river Humber and he readily gave permission to Augustine to carry the gospel across his kingdom. Many pagans were converted to Christianity and while Bede's story that Augustine baptised ten thousand converts on one day is certainly an exaggeration, there is no doubt that the work of evangelism made great advance. Augustine only lived a few years after his arrival in England. He died in 604/605AD, having been earlier consecrated Archbishop of Canterbury. That made Augustine the first Archbishop of the English Church in a line that stretches from Augustine to the present

Archbishop, Rowan Williams. Because Augustine had made Canterbury his headquarters and began building a church there, Canterbury was known as his 'seat.' The Latin word for 'seat' is *cathedra*, hence Canterbury Cathedral.

Down the centuries Canterbury Cathedral has reflected the tides of history in the country. In the 12th century King Henry II took notice of a well-educated young man who was an agent for the Archbishop, Theobald. The young man's name was Thomas Becket (1120-1170). Henry made him Lord Chancellor of England and the two men became close friends. When Theobald died Becket was made Archbishop in 1162. If Henry thought that Becket would do whatever the King wished he was soon disappointed. The courtier turned priest was a man of high principle and made it clear that his first loyalty was to God and not to Henry. In a moment of anger Henry expressed the wish that Becket should be silenced. Four knights took the king at his word, broke their way into the Cathedral and murdered the Archbishop on 29th December 1170. Within months of his death Becket was hailed as a holy martyr and soon pilgrims began to arrive in Canterbury from across England and the Continent to pray at Becket's shrine. There have been many written accounts of Becket's death but none have been so powerful and dramatic as T S Eliot's 1935 work in verse, *Murder in the Cathedral*.

The visit of pilgrims to Canterbury in honour of Thomas Becket is the scene for one of the nation's most famous literary compositions, Geoffrey Chaucer's *The Canterbury Tales*. Chaucer began the work sometime in the 1380s and worked on it for at least ten years. There are sixteen *Tales* in all and a *Prologue*. The *Tales* are stories told by pilgrims walking from Southwark in London to Canterbury, and they are told by a range of people from many walks of life, including a knight, a miller, a merchant, a squire, a physician, a cook, a friar, a nun, etc.

When Henry VIII ordered the dissolution of the monasteries Becket's tomb in Canterbury was destroyed in 1540. The priory was dissolved and many of the monks formed the reconstituted cathedral foundation. These were turbulent times in the land. The Reformation begun by Martin Luther in Germany reached England in the 1520s and for two decades it was tightly controlled by Henry who wanted reform in the Church but not a Reformation. The last Roman Catholic Archbishop of Canterbury was William Warham who died in 1532. Bishop Gregory of Rome had appointed Augustine as Canterbury's first Archbishop and for more than 900 years all Augustine's successors had acknowledged the Pope as Supreme Head of the Church. Now in the 1530s Reformation winds were blowing in England and on Warham's death, Henry appointed Thomas Cranmer as Canterbury's first Reformed Archbishop. In the 17th century England was embroiled in the Civil War between King and Parliament. Oliver Cromwell's parliamentary army smashed much of the Cathedral's stained glass.

So Canterbury remains, not the earliest Christian site in England but one of the earliest. From Augustine to Dr Justin Welby, Canterbury Cathedral has mirrored the highs and lows, the changes, turmoil, Reformation and agitations that have marked Christianity in England for 1400 years.

33. Pilgrim Places

The Christian faith in England has long been associated with places like Glastonbury, Canterbury, York and London. But the town of Whitby, on the north Yorkshire coast, can also lay claim to its own historic Christian roots.

Overlooking a vast expanse of the North Sea, and with its rocky headland and high cliffs, Whitby is one of the favourite seaside attractions in the north east of England. With some narrow winding streets and its associations with Captain James Cook, Whitby has an olde-world feeling about it. High on the headland stand the ruins of St Hilda's Abbey and that's the clue to its link with early British Christianity. Hilda was connected by birth to King Edwin of Northumbria and sometime around 627AD she was converted to the Christian faith. After missionary work in Co Durham, she was appointed by the Christian King Oswy of Northumbria as the first Abbess of the newly-founded Abbey at the place later named Whitby. The Abbey soon had a reputation as a great centre of Christian missions and learning but it was a gathering of royalty, bishops and monks that was to give Whitby lasting fame. The occasion was the Synod of Whitby in 664AD, a gathering of Britain's Christian leaders that would determine the shape of Christianity in these islands until the Reformation. That story, however, begins much earlier.

It would be exciting to know exactly when the Christian faith arrived in these islands and who brought it to us. There have been many suggestions but a very probable answer is that Christian missionaries from Gaul (now France) crossed the English Channel to bring the Good News to our pagan ancestors. A probable date is sometime in the early third century, between 200 and 250AD, thought it might have been considerably earlier. A hundred years later the faith had spread widely and there were Christian settlements in many parts of England and Wales. Ireland was evangelised in the 5th century and, in turn, Irish missionaries took the gospel to Scotland. If we take the year 600AD as our starting point, then we have a picture as follows. The

Celtic Church begun by St Patrick in Ireland was now established in Scotland, spreading out from its centre at Iona. Celtic Christianity was vigorously evangelistic and its monks showed great courage and determination in preaching the gospel and establishing a life style of simple piety, prayer and work. Then in 597AD St Augustine landed in Kent, sent by Bishop Gregory of Rome. Augustine's mission was to make contact with the Christian settlements he knew already existed and persuade them to become a part of the Roman Church he represented.

For 50 years, between 600 and 650AD, these two forms of Christianity were working in England, both engaged in preaching the gospel and building up converts and believers. So we have the older Celtic Christianity now joined by the Roman form of Christianity that came with Augustine. There were no major or important differences between these two organisations. In particular, they were both strongly Trinitarian and they were both committed to preaching the gospel and baptising converts. The differences between them were not in doctrine but rather in organisation and in the celebrations of the Christian year. The Bishop of Canterbury was soon recognised as the Archbishop of all the churches and clergy and monks under his leadership and he, in turn, recognised the Bishop of Rome as his Superior. With the Celtic Church it was different. It also appointed Bishops but it had no Archbishop nor did it see itself in any way a part of the Roman/Canterbury administration. The Celtic Church had been established before Augustine arrived and so it regarded itself as the British Christian Church.

In terms of the Church year the important difference between the two Churches was in their celebration of Easter. The Celtic Church had a tradition which it believed went back to St John and dated Easter in relation to the Jewish Passover. Canterbury Christianity, with its Roman identity, dated Easter differently. While this was not a very important theological difference, it did have practical significance. As with Christians all over the world, British Christians put great importance on Easter and it was the major celebration of the whole

Christian year. Now in Britain this important festival was observed on different dates between the two Christian communities. Celtic Christianity celebrated Easter on one date and Canterbury Christianity on another. This division was particularly noticeable in the household of King Oswy, the very influential King of Northumbria. Among the Celtic Christians kingship was very important and the king was regarded as the anointed of the Lord. In contrast Canterbury Christians recognised the Bishop of Rome, now being called a Pope (from the Latin *papas*, father), as the Head of the Church. To complicate matters further, King Oswy's second wife was a Roman Christian while he was a Celtic Christian. This meant that in the royal household King Oswy could be celebrating Easter while the queen and her attendants were observing the Lenten Fast!

Finally King Oswy decided that this question of the date of Easter must be settled once and for all. He called a Synod of both Celtic and Roman Christians and the meeting place was Whitby Abbey where Hilda was the greatly esteemed Abbess. The two parties arrived to take part in the Synod; the Celtic monks and priests and the Canterbury clergy. They were easily distinguished from each other by their hairstyles! The Celts had adopted the tonsure, shaving the crowns of their heads but the Roman clergy did not adopt this custom. Colman, bishop of Lindisfarne, led the Celtic monks, supported by Irish and Scottish monks and Hilda. The Roman deputation was led by Agilbert, bishop of Dorchester, Wilfrid, abbot of Ripon, and James the deacon. King Oswy presided and none of those attending that gathering in Whitby could have foreseen the long-term outcome of the proceedings.

Colman argued that the Celtic tradition went back through Columba, who brought the gospel to Iona, Polycarp, bishop and martyr in the 2nd century, and the Apostle John. Wilfrid, the Roman spokesman, said their tradition was now accepted by Christians all over Europe and that it could be traced back to the teaching of both Peter and Paul. Argument and counter-argument followed. Colman and his supporters emphasised that John was the Lord's beloved disciple and that his teaching therefore carried great weight. Wilfrid, an ambitious young cleric, suggested that the Celtic Church was confused in its calculations and that it was time for the obstinate Irish and Scottish monks to forsake their out-of-date practices and join 'the universal Church.' He then added very pointedly that Peter had the keys to heaven and it was unwise to ignore his tradition. This alarmed King Oswy who asked Colman if our Lord had indeed given the keys of heaven to Peter. Colman said yes because it was recorded in Matthew's gospel. That decided the matter for King Oswy. Without asking what the 'keys of heaven' meant, Oswy declared that he and his people would follow St Peter and the Roman tradition. He would not offend the apostle who controlled the gates of heaven!

The die was cast! A momentous decision had been made at the Synod of Whitby. King Oswy committed himself and his country to the Roman tradition. Hilda accepted the decision but Colman resigned as Bishop of Lindisfarne and with many of his monks returned to Iona. Of course the Celtic Church did not disappear immediately but after Whitby, the Roman Church in Britain was in the ascendancy. Celtic Christianity remained in these islands for another three centuries but was eventually incorporated with the more powerful and prestigious Roman administration. The Synod of Whitby committed the British Church to the jurisdiction of Rome and the Pope. That jurisdiction lasted for eight hundred years until it was challenged and dismantled by the Reformation.

34. Pilgrim Places

Thirty-five miles south west of Belfast in Northern Ireland, among the rolling fields of Co Armagh, stands the city of Armagh. The pride of the city is its famous cathedral, St Patrick's Church of Ireland Cathedral. While Belfast is the capital city of Northern Ireland and Dublin of Southern Ireland, Armagh is the undisputed ecclesiastical capital of the whole country. High on a hill in the city stands the Cathedral named after Ireland's patron saint, Patrick. According to tradition it was Patrick who caused the first church building to be erected on this hill more than 1500 years ago. Dublin, New York and Melbourne in Australia also have their own Cathedrals named after Patrick. So who was this Patrick who has cathedrals in his memory and after whom so many families around the word have named a son Patrick?

Patrick was a 5th century monk but his exact dates are uncertain. Although Ireland has long claimed him as the country's saint, one of the few things we know for certain about him is that he was not born in Ireland. He was born c.400 and his home was most likely somewhere on the Firth of Clyde in Scotland. We know from his own writings that he was brought up in a Christian home and that his father, Calpornius, was a deacon and his grandfather, Potitus, a priest. When he was about sixteen years of age his village was attacked by Irish raiders and he was carried off to Ireland. He was sold as a slave in Co Antrim and was put to work tending cattle. During the next six years he prayed daily and experienced a spiritual conversion. He escaped from captivity, travelled nearly two hundred miles and then boarded a ship. Eventually he made his way back home to his family. A few years later he had a vision in which he felt he was being called back to Ireland. Believing he had heard the voice of God he returned to the land where he had been a slave and preached the gospel there until his death.

Such, in outline, is Patrick's life. There are no certain dates and although we have his *Confession*, a kind of autobiography, it has many gaps. It is fairly certain that he was ordained to the priesthood but he doesn't tell us where this took place or who ordained him. He never mentions the Roman Church, there are no reference to the Bishop of Rome and there is no indication that any Roman church or bishop sent him to preach in Ireland. The *Confession* is written in rather poor Latin and it is clear that Patrick had little or no theological education. However, he loved God with all his heart and he longed to spread the gospel among the pagan Irish. From the beginning his ministry was wonderfully blessed of God. He saw many pagans converted to Christianity and he writes that he baptised thousands of converts. He travelled in most parts of Ireland and as the work developed he ordained some of the converts as Christian priests. He witnessed before kings and chieftains and won great respect among the people.

Patrick founded and established the Celtic form of Christianity in Ireland and after his death Irish Celtic monks like Columba and Aidan carried it to Scotland and northeast England. Because of the later disputes and divisions that arose in British Christianity, it is important to note the characteristics of the Celtic Christianity that Patrick established. Celtic teaching was strongly Trinitarian, accepted the Scriptures as God's Word and emphasised the doctrines of sin, grace, repentance, new birth, holy living, resurrection and final judgement. It also emphasised a simple life style and was strongly missionary-minded. Patrick's mission and work in Ireland was completely independent and he never refers to the Roman Church or the Bishop of Rome. His call to be a missionary in Ireland had come directly from God. For these reasons the 8th century historian, Venerable Bede, never once mentions Patrick in his *Ecclesiastical History of the English People*. Although Patrick's mission lasted at least forty years and although he evangelised Ireland and built churches and monasteries, Bede completely ignored him. The reason for this is clear. Bede was the historian, spokesman and champion of Roman Christianity in Britain and Patrick was no part of that establishment.

Although the exact date is not known, it was probably sometime in the 460s that Patrick built a simple church on the hill in Armagh where his cathedral now stands. It is a fitting reminder of that good and godly missionary who, with his monks and those who followed in the next centuries, achieved so much in the evangelisation of Ireland. When he died he left behind many thousands of baptised Christians and a growing number of zealous monks to carry on the work. Patrick's work and influence later reached Scotland though Columba and England through Aidan. Like most of the events in his life, Patrick's death cannot be dated with certainty. A date in the 480s or 90s is likely. He was buried some forty miles from where St Patrick's cathedral now stands, in the town of Downpatrick, so named after his resting place.

So what kind of man was Patrick and what motivated him? The only sure evidence we have is the three pieces of writing he left behind him; the *Confession,* a *Letter*, and the *Lorica*, a hymn known as Patrick's Breastplate. In the centuries following his death, Patrick's reputation as a saint grew and *Lives* of Patrick began to appear. Each new *Life* tried to out-do its predecessors by recording more and more miracles that Patrick is supposed to have performed. Frankly these medieval 'biographies' and the modern versions based on them are worthless. They are crammed full of medieval myth and superstition and the glorified super Roman saint they portray is far removed from the genuine Patrick. In the *Confession* we see the true Patrick; humble, devoted to God and giving his whole life to preach the gospel in the pagan land he adopted as home. Compared with the scores of 'miracles' that appear in the medieval biographies, Patrick records only one kind of miracle – the miracle of pagan men and women converted to faith in Christ. Whether or not he plucked a small plant from the ground and used its three leaves (the shamrock) to illustrate the Trinity, he worshipped the Father, Son and Holy Spirit. In the familiar words translated from his Breastplate, he faced pagan powers and the demonic spirits behind them, strong in his Trinitarian faith.

> I bind unto myself today
> The strong Name of the Trinity
> By invocation of the same
> The Three in One, and One in Three.

In short, Patrick was a New Testament Christian, an evangelical Christian. He loved the Scriptures and his *Confession* is full of Scripture quotations and references. His preaching and ministry converted pagans to Christ and at his death Ireland had many Christian people, churches and settlements. In the following centuries Celtic Christianity was characterised both by its devotion to learning and its passion for mission. It was this heritage, springing from Patrick's life and work, that gave Ireland the description, 'the land of saints and scholars.' Today, looking east and west and north and south from Patrick's Cathedral high on Armagh hill, is to be reminded of the humble monk who planted the Christian faith on this island. Patrick, like Barnabas, was 'a good man, full of the Holy Spirit' (Acts 11:24). It was not a Pope, or a bishop, or a Church council or any ecclesiastical recognition that made Patrick the Apostle of Ireland; rather it was his supreme devotion to Christ and the gospel.

35. Pilgrim Places

Off the end of the Mull peninsula in the Inner Hebrides in Scotland lies a small island, Iona. It is situated a mile from the mainland and is little more than three miles in length and one mile in width. While it is very likely that Ninian (died c.430) brought Christianity to southwest Scotland around the year 400, we have much better historical records for what happened at Iona. In 563 a boat arrived at the island bringing a group of monks from Ireland. They had braved the storms of the Atlantic Ocean since leaving the Irish coast and their arrival in Iona began a new chapter in the history of Scottish Christianity. Their arrival would also have important consequences for English Christianity.

The monks were led by Columba. He was born in county Donegal, in the northwest of Ireland, probably sometime in the 520s. By birth he was connected to Irish kings and he was schooled and trained in Celtic Christianity. Patrick had founded the Celtic faith in Ireland in the previous century and Columba was one of a number of outstanding monks and scholars that the Celtic Church produced. Although the details are uncertain, Columba became involved in controversy about biblical manuscripts with another Celtic scholar, Finnian, who headed a monastery at Clonard. If the traditions can be believed, this controversy led to a local war and soldiers were killed. Columba was judged to be in the wrong and he was forced into exile. With some fellow monks, he left Ireland by boat, bound for Scotland, and landed at Iona.

It was indeed a momentous event. Although there is evidence that Ninian had evangelised parts of southwest Scotland, the inhabitants of the country, the Picts, were pagans when Columba arrived. For the next forty years Columba and his monks travelled and preached and catechised and evangelised much of the south and west of Scotland. Iona was their headquarters and Columba founded an abbey there. The little island was soon recognised as a centre both of Christian spirituality and Christian learning. In Columba's lifetime and in the centuries following, Iona, in spite of its isolation, became a place of pilgrimage. Columba and his monks established churches and monasteries, ordained priests and appointed monks according to the Celtic faith and customs they had learned in Ireland. Columba was a man of many gifts and talents. He was a preacher, an evangelist, a translator, a scholar and a diplomat. The Pict chieftains respected him and he travelled freely across the country. Traditions about him recount how the tribal chiefs consulted him not only about the faith he preached, but about the education and care of their people and also political matters.

There are two main accounts of Columba's life and work. About a hundred years after his death one of the Abbots of Iona, Adomnan, wrote *Vita Columbae*, 'Life of Columba,' and Bede, in his *Ecclesiastical History of the English People*, also gave information about him. While both these sources are informative and fascinating, it is often difficult to separate the fact from the fiction. Many miracles are attributed to Columba and its simply not possible to tell what great works were wrought by Columba in the power of the Spirit and what 'miracles' were invented by sympathetic biographers and historians. What is not in doubt, however, is that Columba was a man of God and while there are questions about how many physical miracles he performed, there is no question at all that another kind of miracle authenticated Columba's ministry. This was what might be called the ever-present miracle of the gospel of Christ; lives changed from darkness to light and from sin to holiness by the transforming power of the regenerating Holy Spirit. Columba made a visit back to Ireland late in life and returned to finish his days on his beloved Iona. He died there on June 9th, 597, and was buried in the abbey he had founded. It is worth noting that the year in which Columba died on the Scottish island of Iona, 597, was also the year in which Augustine arrived in Kent to bring Roman Christianity to England.

While the Celtic Christianity that flourished at Iona succeeded in evangelising large parts of Scotland, its influence also reached England. In the 1630s, Oswald was King of Northumbria. He had visited Iona at least once and was very impressed with the Christian community there. Oswald was a baptised Christian and he was concerned about the evangelisation of the pagans in his kingdom. He wanted a strong, missionary-minded evangelical bishop to oversee the Church in Northumbria and he asked Iona for help. The monks at Iona asked Aidan, bishop of Scattery Island at the mouth of the river Shannon in the west of Ireland, to go to Northumbria. Aidan consented and in the year 635 he arrived in the northeast of England. He made his home on the island of Lindisfarne (Holy Island) but set up his episcopal centre at nearby Bamburgh on the mainland. King Oswald warmly welcomed Aidan and the two men became firm friends. Oswald gave Aidan every possible help and encouragement and Aidan began a ministry of visitation, preaching, teaching and evangelism that was to result in Northumbria being the most Christianised of all the provinces in England. It was the 19th century Bishop Lightfoot of Durham, famed scholar and historian, who said that England's real patron saint was neither St George or Augustine of Canterbury but Aidan of Lindisfarne. This judgement can hardly be challenged. Aidan not only made Northumbria a great centre of Celtic Christianity but the example of his loving, humble and sacrificial ministry inspired his fellow clergy and many more in the centuries following.

When Aidan died in 651AD, he had, with the help of his clergy and monks, not only evangelised Northumbria but also he had taken Celtic Christianity to other parts of England. Lindisfarne had become the English form of what Columba had first established on Iona. Celtic Christianity, in Iona and Lindisfarne, had always traced its roots to St John and Asia Minor. It was on another island, Patmos, that John received the visions and revelations found in the last book of the Bible, the Book of Revelation. On Scotland's island of Iona and England's island of Lindisfarne, the Johannine tradition of Christianity, in the form of Celtic Christianity, flourished. Having lighted the fires of authentic New Testament Christianity in Ireland with the life and work of Patrick, the sparks of Celtic spirituality were carried first to Iona and later to Lindisfarne.

In 1938, a year before Europe was plunged into the horrors of World War II, the Rev Dr George MacLeod founded the Iona Community. He took a party of working men from Glasgow to rebuild the ruined medieval Iona Abbey. It was the beginning of a project to make Iona a spiritual retreat. The Iona Community has grown in reputation across the decades as it seeks to interpret and apply the gospel in the contemporary world. So for about 1450 years the Christian faith has been established on this little Hebridean island. As the prophet asked, 'Who has despised the day of small things?' (Zech. 4:10). When Columba and his fellow monks pulled their little boat ashore on Iona in 563AD, it appeared indeed to be a day of small importance. But God was with them and, using the Bible's metaphor of spiritual fire, the sparks kindled on Iona brought the light of the gospel to the pagan darkness of Scotland and England.

36. John Wesley's Social Activism

The Wesleyan Revival in 18th century Britain had wide repercussions on the population, both spiritually and in improving social conditions. When John and Charles Wesley began their itinerant preaching work in 1739, there was much social deprivation in the country. Poverty was endemic, drunkenness and mob violence was commonplace, and there was no organised police force. John Wesley saw 'Methodism' as raised up by God to 'reform the Church and the nation and to spread scriptural holiness over the land.' The consequences of the revival were not only that thousands of people found personal salvation, but also social conditions noticeably improved.

This social activism arose from John Wesley's understanding of what genuine Christianity is; the love of God and neighbour. Throughout his long ministry he constantly referred to the words of Jesus in Matthew 22:37-40 as a summary of how God expects His people to live. 'You shall love the Lord your God with all your heart …soul … mind … [and] your neighbour as yourself.' Wesley preached that saving grace is transforming grace. The Christian becomes an influence for good and for holiness among the people he influences. This is what Wesley meant by 'reforming the Church and the nation.' The 'Methodists' were to be both salt and light in the land. Holy people would radiate holy influence and the love described by Paul in 1 Corinthians 13 is the love that is produced by true faith. Wesley was equally fond of quoting Galatians 5:6 that union with Christ means 'faith working through love.' The Wesleyan revival emphasised that we are not saved *by* our good works but we are saved *for* good works.

John Wesley's own ministry set the example for this kind of holy living that involved itself in serving others. He gathered his people together in local areas into groups called 'Societies.' The only condition of membership in these Methodist Societies was a person's 'desire to save their soul and flee from the wrath to come.' Weekly class meetings were organised which were made up of eleven members and a leader. Each member was asked to contribute one penny a week into the common fund. This money was not primarily to pay for the 'preaching houses' that the Methodists were building; instead it was to help poor people in that area. All his life John Wesley had a deep concern to help the poor and the money raised in the Societies was used to alleviate poverty.

Wesley's next social enterprise was to open an orphanage in Newcastle in the north east of England. Visiting Newcastle he had seen the many homeless children wandering the streets and living by begging and stealing. The orphanage was organised as a refuge for these poor children and the staff, hand-picked by Wesley, gave them shelter, clothing, food and school lessons. Here indeed was the love of God in action. The children were cared for in every way and the orphanage became their home until they were old enough to take care of themselves.

John Wesley then turned his attention to help educate the children of the poor. Children from wealthy homes could attend the growing number of private schools or even have a teacher instruct them at home. But what about the children of the poor? In Bristol, where Wesley's itinerant ministry began in 1739, he saw the hundreds of poor children who had no chance at all of receiving even a basic education. Eventually three Methodist schools were opened in Bristol, two of them for the children of the poor and one for the sons and daughters of his preachers. While it was not possible for Wesley and his Methodist people to open schools and orphanages all over the country, yet they were doing what they could to relieve poverty long before Government agencies were organised to do this on a national scale. And it should not be forgotten that the world's first-ever Sunday School was organised in 1769 by Hannah Ball, a Methodist class leader, in High Wycombe, a town situated forty miles west of London.

As he travelled the land Wesley saw that the plight of the poor was particularly desperate when they were ill. They had no money to give to a doctor, so many died simply because they could not afford any medical help. Wesley's response to this everyday tragedy was to open a free dispensary in London. He provided free medical advice and basic medicines for those who otherwise would have died. This was the first free medical dispensary ever opened in England. Some years later Wesley donated his own money to set up a loan scheme from which poor people could borrow small sums of money without having to pay any interest. In another move to help the poor, he employed some women to work on cotton being prepared for manufacture. This employment enabled then to earn a small income to help feed and clothe their families.

While none of these schemes to help the poor inaugurated a social revolution in England, they were genuine attempts by Wesley and his people to help the poor. This was what Wesley meant by loving his neighbour; holiness is love in action. Holiness is not just the repetition of correct theological formulations, nor is it just words about Christian responsibility. For John Wesley the love of neighbour is, in the summary of his principles written after his death: 'Do all the good you can, to all the people you can, in all the ways you can, for as long as you can.' A number of historians have claimed that the Wesleyan revival saved England from the kind of blood-letting revolution that convulsed France in 1789. The social and political conditions, however, in England and France, were markedly different. While the poor in both countries felt forgotten by their governments and were resentful in their helplessness, England had not witnessed the violent anti-government and anti-royalist anger that pushed the French into open rebellion. The English populace were not exposed to the yawning gaps that existed between the aristocracy and the poor in France, and so there was less incentive to rebellion. While the Wesleyan revival perhaps cannot be credited with saving Britain from a French-type revolution, yet it is undeniable that it was a powerful force for social improvement. As thousands of people were reached with the gospel of Christ and saved from their old sinful lifestyles, their changed social behaviour was like salt purifying the nation. The 'Methodists' were sober, hard working and politically conservative. Such people would not resort to political executions and brutal revolution. They feared God, respected authority, worked hard and loved their neighbours.

The foundation for this life-style was the Christian gospel brought to them in the Wesleyan revival.

The various schemes that John Wesley and his people set in motion to relieve poverty and lessen social injustices did not bring an instant Utopia. They were however, leavening influences that contributed to a more caring and compassionate society. Wesley pointed the way, in the practical love of neighbour, that governments would adopt and implement in the generations to come. While, however, these Methodist charities were limited in their immediate success, there was one notable exception. John Wesley was the first English Christian leader who plainly and forcefully opposed slavery in the British Empire. His powerful 1774 tract, *Thoughts upon Slavery*, condemned slavery as contrary, not only to the Christian love of neighbour, but to common humanity. While the combined powers of Church and State argued that slavery was an economic necessity, Wesley thundered that it could never be reconciled with love of neighbour. He gave strong support to William Wilberforce, Christian and philanthropist, who was finally successful in 1807 in winning parliamentary support to abolish slavery. John Wesley spent his long life in what he described as 'spreading scriptural holiness over the land.' At the heart of the Wesleyan revival lay the conviction that while holiness is loving God with all our hearts, it is no less loving our neighbour as ourselves.

37. In The Depth Of The Sea

(Micah 7:19). The Bible is very expressive when it comes to speaking about how God can forgive our sins. It uses many descriptions to tell us how our sins are both forgiven and forgotten. Here is a sample of these great promises. Our sins are 'forgiven,' (Ps. 32:5); 'washed thoroughly' and 'blotted out' (Ps. 51:2, 9); 'forgiven and covered' (Ps. 85:2); 'washed whiter than snow' (Is. 1:18); 'taken away' (Is. 6:7); 'put behind His back' (Is. 38:17); 'laid on Him' (Is. 53:6); 'remembered no more' (Jer. 31:34); 'pardoned' (Jer. 33:8); 'destroyed' (Rom. 6:6); 'purged' (Heb. 1:3)' 'borne for us' (1 Pet. 2:24); 'washed away' (Rev. 1:5).

What glorious news this is! In Christ we are truly forgiven! Our sins are cancelled! God will not hold our guilty past against us! The prophet Micah has a very dramatic way of telling us this. He says that God has cast our sins 'into the depths of the sea' (7:19). So how deep is the sea? Far out in the Western Pacific Ocean, two hundred miles from the island of Guam, lies the deepest part of the earth's oceans. It is called the Mariana Trench. It is more than 1500 miles long and over 40 miles wide but it is its depth that is awesome. It plunges down into the ocean bed for some 35,800 feet. By comparison, Everest, the world's highest mountain, is 29,000 feet in height. That means that the Mariana Trench goes lower into the ocean bed than the peak of Everest stretches up to the clouds. At that frightening depth the pressure from the waters above is more than 8 tons to the square inch!

While these geographical facts and figures compel our attention, the theology of our forgiveness is even more wonderful! When we are 'in Christ' as His redeemed people, our sins are truly forgiven. God has thrown them into the depth of the sea, never to be resurrected! They are buried forever in the vast abyss of God's unfathomable love and mercy. What great, good news the gospel brings! Our guilty past is both forgiven and forgotten! A few months after his evangelical conversion in May 1738, John Wesley went to Herrnhut in Germany. He wanted to see the headquarters of the Moravians, the German

Christians who had helped him so much in his search for spiritual assurance. He met the Moravian hymn writer Johann Andreas Rothe. Wesley had learned Germany and enjoyed singing the Moravian hymns. He translated many of them into English, including one of Rothe's great hymns that begins:

> Now I have found the ground wherein
> Sure my soul's anchor may remain...

One of the verses expresses the biblical teaching on how our sins are forever lost in the vast ocean of God's forgiving love.

> O Love, Thou bottomless abyss
> My sins are swallowed up in Thee
> Covered is my unrighteousness
> Nor spot of guilt remains on me.
> While Jesu's blood through earth and skies
> Mercy, free boundless mercy, cries.

38. On The Damascus Road

Martin Luther (1483-1546) occupies a very large place in Church History. He made a major contribution to a Reformation in the Medieval Church in the 16th century and there some 60 million Christians today who call themselves Lutherans. In addition the millions of Christians who call themselves Protestants can trace their origins, in the main, to the Reformation born from Luther's re-discovery of the true gospel. Born in Eisleben in Germany, Luther's parents had high hopes for him to study law but instead he entered a monastery. In spite of concentrated study, long prayers and vigils, Luther could not find peace with God. When his Augustinian Order sent him as a delegate to Rome, he spent his time visiting and praying at every shrine and church in the 'Eternal City.' He returned to Wittenberg University, was awarded a Doctor of Theology degree and began to lecture on the books of the Bible. It was his careful study of the biblical text that was to give him the longed-for sense of forgiveness, and set him on a career of teaching, preaching, publishing and supporting a Reformation that would change the history of Europe.

In his room in the tower of the university Luther poured over his books as he prepared lectures on the book of Romans. He was puzzled and deeply disturbed by Romans 1:17. 'In it [the gospel] the righteousness of God is revealed through faith for faith.' Luther pondered on the words 'the righteousness of God.' What is this righteousness? Does it mean that God is righteous? Luther already knew that God was righteous while he was a miserable sinner. Did it mean that God demanded him to be righteous? Well that was not good news for Luther knew he was not righteous. He continued to study the text, comparing scripture with scripture and consulting the writings of the Church Fathers. Then the great moment came. 'I grasped the truth that the righteousness of God is that righteousness whereby, through grace and sheer mercy, he justifies us by faith. Thereupon I felt myself to be reborn and to have gone through open doors into paradise.' Martin Luther had found the true gospel! He had discovered in Paul's letter to the Romans that God justifies us, not by works, or merit, or endeavour, or right belief, or religious practice – but by faith in Christ who died for us. And this great discovery was not merely theological or academic. It was personal. There among his books Luther found the personal forgiveness of his sins, acceptance with God and deep peace in his soul. Luther's conversion was a truly Damascus Road experience. Like Paul before him, it launched him on the great passion of his life - promoting the gospel of salvation by grace alone through faith alone.

39. Passover Sensation In Jewish Capital

"Never a Passover like it." "Unheard of in Jerusalem before." "Galilean hysterics." These and like expressions have been on multitudes of lips at this annual feast, for Jerusalem has witnessed the most unusual and startling Passover in its long history.

Part of the mystery is that no one seems to know exactly what has happened. As with all crowds, some say one thing and some another. In the last few days I have interviewed scores of people and the result is baffling. Certainly, a few of those questioned were adamant and not a little aggressive in asserting that nothing whatever had happened. The priests were particularly scornful about the whole affair. But a far greater number were more or less convinced that strange happenings were undeniable.

Accounts Garbled

The accounts were garbled, confused, and contradictory. But two observations in particular keep reappearing: first, an account of a country prophet, believing himself Messiah, crucified by the Romans and now said to have risen from the dead; and, second, a startling rumour, neither confirmed nor denied by the priests, that the great curtain of the holy place in the Temple was suddenly ripped from top to bottom on the Passover eve.

On sifting the accounts of many witnesses, the story seems to be this. For a number of years, Jerusalem and many of the neighbouring towns and villages have witnessed strange scenes through the preaching of a layman from Nazareth. Reports have it that in spite of the large crowds he drew, this peasant-prophet had had no rabbinical training. Indeed, many assert that before taking to the road, he was a carpenter.

There have been plenty of stories of strange scenes and "miracles"— of lunatics healed, cripples made to walk, the blind to see—and one fantastic account of a man in Bethany raised from the dead! The priests soon put a stop to that rumour.

This was going on for some time, in spite of sporadic opposition from the Jewish leaders, and nothing might have come of it had it not been for an incident last week.

Roman Guards Doubled

This preacher, called Jesus, had by now a large following. Multitudes declared him to be Israel's Messiah and deliverer, the great prophet long promised. On the other hand, there was a multitude equally vocal in emphatically denying this, including most of the priests and men of letters. To them, this Jesus from Nazareth was an impostor, one more in a line of many deceived into thinking they were Messiah.

Two weeks ago, Nisan 10, this carpenter-preacher entered Jerusalem on a donkey, followed by great, excited, clamouring, shouting crowd of followers. The Romans immediately doubled the guards, well knowing the explosive nature of Jewish crowds. Jesus, however, showed no signs of firing the popular enthusiasm. Instead, he slipped quietly away to the Temple—and there it happened.

Denounces Bazaar

It wasn't a religious speech, political harangue, or "miracle" that started things moving, but an attack by Jesus—a physical assault in the Temple courtyard. This place, known here as "The Court of the Gentiles," was filled with traders doing a roaring business with the many pilgrims that crowded the city. The exchangers were there too, changing foreign coins into Jewish currency. Only the latter, of course, is acceptable in the Temple treasury. Apparently Jesus watched this for a while and then went to work. With a whip, said by some to have been made on the spot, He routed the traders and money changers, tipped up their tables, and overthrew their stalls. Next he drove out the cattle and sheep and ordered the caged pigeons and turtledoves removed. His reasons? With blazing eyes and strong invective, reminiscent of an Elijah some said, the carpenter-turned-reformer rebuked those whom he denounced as turning God's house into a bazaar. The result was uproar. The priests were furious. One report has it that Caiaphas, the high priest, on hearing the news, swore that this time the impostor had gone too far.

Problems with Witnesses

No one is quite sure of what happened after that. By the Passover eve, Nisan 14, Jesus had been arrested and his followers scattered. The charges brought against him were three: (1) blasphemy against the law; (2) pretending to be Messiah; and (3) exciting the populace to revolt against Rome, saying he was the true king of the Jews.

One cannot but feel that the last charge was a desperate attempt to pin something on him. The Jews are always grumbling against Rome, and have never for a moment recognized Caesar as their king.

The Sanhedrin not only had trouble with the charges, but with the witnesses as well. What a mixed crew it was! A Jerusalem lawyer and a swarthy money changer, a fumbling old scribe from Bethany and a vigorous orator from somewhere in the north, generally reputed to be a leader in the underground rebel movement, the Zealots. Other witnesses included merchants, priests, and a half-dozen fellows one can only describe as riffraff. Some say that one Judas, a former follower of the prophet, was also there.

Prisoner Silent

The Sanhedrin, in spite of all its questioning, examination, and cross-examination, found it difficult to establish any of the charges. No two witnesses seemed to agree on anything and it was all too evident that many of them were hired to testify against the preacher. Finally, when it looked as though the accusations might fail, Caiaphas, in a fit of rage, flung aside his robe, declaring the imposter had condemned himself. But others were not so sure. The prisoner said very little.

Immediately after, Jesus was sent to the governor, Pilate. There are confused reports of what happened then. Many believe that Pilate, at first, wanted to let the prisoner go free. But the crowds in the street, made vocal by the priests, howled that such an act would be treason against Rome.

A few hours later the prophet, in company with two thieves, was led out to a hill, known locally as Calvary, and there crucified. Multitudes gathered to watch the grim procession but there were no attempts to free the prisoners. The awful work completed, the people began to drift away, thinking it was all over.

Big Blackout

In fact, things had just begun. Although it was only midday, a sudden darkness filled the sky, blotting out the sun and making people stumble and fall in their frantic fear and rush to get home. Of all the strange happenings, real or imaginary, reputed to have taken place, the mystery of the darkness I saw for myself. In my room, off the Damascus Road, I finished my dispatches by candlelight.

When the darkness finally cleared at about three in the afternoon, what a commotion there was! A great earthquake near the Calvary hill had rent the ground into great fissures. But that was not all. Far from it! People rushed through the street screaming they had seen ghosts. Apparently it began with discovering that the earthquake had disturbed a burial place and men and women, clearly petrified with fear, whispered of having seen the dead walking! All was confusion and consternation.

Then, to add the last touch, a young Temple priest ran among the crowd, tearing his hair and jabbering that judgment was about to fall. On being calmed down, he gasped to a dumb-struck crowd the incredible news that the great curtain of the holy place, the most feared and sacred thing in all Jerusalem, was mysteriously ripped from top to bottom. Ordinary priests, he wailed, had looked into the "holiest." What could now prevent the wrath of Heaven?

Probe Empty Grave

On the third day it happened—the most shattering and unbelievable part of this whole fantastic affair. Things were beginning to settle down as before when a rumour spread like wildfire that the Nazarene prophet had disappeared—his grave was empty! Expecting some mischief from his followers and tipped off by the Jewish leaders, the Romans had placed sentries by the tomb. Now the centurion was sent to investigate. What a sight he and the soldiers saw! The great stone was rolled away from the mouth of the grave, which was now empty. All around, as though struck by an invisible hand, the guards lay unconscious, with fear frozen on their faces. Of the prophet's body, there was no trace. He had vanished.

Many of his followers, in hiding since he was arrested, now suddenly appeared—claiming to have seen their leader, risen and fully alive. Two of them, going home to the nearby village of Emmaus, rushed back to Jerusalem, declaring excitedly that they had met Jesus and that he had dined with them! Others speak of seeing him at different times, and all of them confidently assert it is the same prophet and preacher from Nazareth, alive from the dead! As expected, the Jewish leaders flatly deny the whole thing, speaking of it as a hoax, practised by the prophet's followers.

I, with many others, just don't know. But thinking of all that happened, especially the darkness, I wonder if it was a hoax. Could it be true? Really true? What if? One thing is sure: this Passover, Jerusalem will never forget.

40. But God!

In the story of Joseph in the book of Genesis there is a passage near the end that illustrates how God works in our lives and circumstances in the most remarkable ways. When Jacob died, his sons feared that their brother Joseph would exact vengeance for the evil they had done to him. When they knelt before Joseph, now a great lord in Egypt, they feared the worst. Joseph's reply was generous and magnanimous. 'You meant evil against me, **but God** meant it for good' (Gen. 50:20). Both halves of this sentence tell a great story. The first half, 'You meant evil against me' is a reminder of family favouritism and jealousies that had tragic consequences. Jacob's preferential love for his son Joseph made the boy proud and arrogant and his brothers' jealousy turned to revenge. They sold him to passing desert traders and told their father that a wild beast had killed him. Joseph was sold into slavery in Egypt but his wise counsel and good conduct made him a valued servant to Potiphar, an Egyptian general. His refusal to compromise with Potiphar's wife landed him in gaol and even when his predictions for others proved true, he was kept in prison.

Brought before the Pharaoh, Joseph's interpretation of dreams brought him release and rapid promotion. When the famine he had predicted struck Egypt, he was made virtually Prime Minister in the land and his scheme of storing crops saved the land. His eleven brothers came to Egypt to buy corn and although Joseph recognised them, they did not recognise him. Later, when he discovered that his father was still alive, he told his shocked brothers who he was. They trembled with fear but Joseph was not planning revenge. As he looked back over the hard years of being a slave and in prison, he saw the hand of God in all of it. 'You meant evil against me,' he told his brothers,' '**but God** meant it for good.' '**But God**'! How precious, how wonderful, how providential, how reassuring those two words are! Against all the odds, God was working on Joseph's behalf. In spite of his brothers' cruel hatred, in spite of Potiphar's wife's dangerous solicitations, in spite of being forgotten by those he befriended in prison, Joseph triumphed because through it all God was on his side! **But God!** is a glowing testimony to God's great plans and purposes for His people. Its New Testament equivalent is when Paul says that 'in everything God works for good for those who love him' (Romans 8:28). The Sovereign Lord of earth and heaven, of time and eternity, of life and death, holds His people secure in every circumstance. One day when we will look back on our lives and on all the things that baffle us now, and often cause us hurt and pain and anguish and doubt, we will say with Joseph, and Paul, and all who have travelled the road of faith – '**but God** meant it for good.'

41. John Wesley And The Salvation Of Souls

John Wesley (1703-1791) began to preach the gospel at Bristol to those outside the Church on Monday, 2nd April, 1739, and he finished on the 7th of October, 1790, at Winchelsea, Sussex. Between these two he covered the country in fifty-one years. Beginning with the 'heart warming' in 1738, he began to preach around London. 'The word of God ran as fire among stubble ... Multitudes crying out, "What must I do to be saved?"' In the half-century, he would preach in every corner of England, Ireland, Wales and Scotland, and the Lord did not slacken His place. In Bristol Wesley was summoned by the Bishop, Joseph Butler, and told in no uncertain terms that he had no business preaching there. Wesley replied. 'My business on earth is to do what good I can. ... A dispensation of the gospel is committed to me, and woe is me if I preach not the gospel.' These telling phrases describe John Wesley as a man with a mission, even if that offended a bishop of the Established Church.

Wesley was totally committed to the great ministry of gospel preaching. On his first visit to Epworth, he preached every morning at the village green and every evening on his father's tombstone. The crowd filled the churchyard to hear the gospel delivered by the preacher who had once been curate in the church. Wesley commented. 'I did far more good to them by preaching three days on my father's tomb than I did to them in my father's pulpit.' He preached without notes, holding the Bible in his hand. We could label his favourite passages as evangelistic texts. In his preaching he emphasised sin, grace, repentance, the new birth and the witness of the Spirit. From Inverness in the north of Scotland to the southern tip of Cornwall, from Lincoln to Limerick in the west of Ireland, he called sinners to repentance.

For 50 years John Wesley's passion for evangelism never abated. He travelled and preached and pleaded with sinners right to the end of his life. He preached his final sermon just seven days before he died. Forty-six years earlier he had counselled his preachers. 'You have nothing to do but save souls. Therefore spend and be spent in this work. And go always, not only to those who want you, but to those who want you most.' Nothing to do but save souls! These words are a biography of John Wesley.

42. Because He Lives I Can Face Tomorrow

The New Testament not only reminds us that Christ rose from the dead on the first Easter morning, but it also reminds us that His resurrection is the guarantee of our salvation. Paul could hardly say it more plainly. 'If Christ has not been raised, your faith is futile and you are still in your sins' (1 Cor. 15:17). But that is not all. Paul adds that if Christ still lies in the tomb then all those who died in the Christian faith have perished and the gospel offers no more hope than the pagan cults. He gives the same emphasis to Christ's resurrection when he writes to the Roman Christians. Our Lord was 'put to death for our sins and raised for our justification' (Rom. 4:25). Salvation is offered to all who sincerely confess that Jesus is Lord and who believe 'that God raised him from the dead' (Rom. 10:9). Faith in our Lord's resurrection is not peripheral to the Christian gospel; it is absolutely foundational. Abraham, Moses, Confucius, Mohammed and all the religious leaders of every age and creed are all dead – Christ alone rose from the dead and lives for ever. Only the Christian gospel has an Easter Day!

And from the first Easter Day comes the story of the Emmaus Road and how two disciples were transformed when they discovered their Lord was alive. Luke recounts the event in some detail (24:13-35). Two disciples, one named Cleopas, were returning from Jerusalem to Emmaus on that Easter evening. As yet they did not know that their Lord was risen and they were downcast and desolate. When a stranger joined them on the road they told him of the mighty works that Jesus of Nazareth had done, for 'he was a prophet mighty in deed and word.' Then they added 'We had hoped ...it is now the third day.' 'We had hoped.' Having been eyewitnesses of our Lord's ministry, they were sure He must be the Messiah. But it had all gone wrong. He had been arrested, falsely accused and crucified. Now his body lay in Joseph's tomb and three days had come and gone. How they had hoped! Hoped for a sign, hoped for a miracle, hoped that somehow God would intervene, but nothing happened. They were going home, sad, disconsolate and with so many memories.

They invited the stranger into their home and as he broke bread they suddenly realised it was the Lord! He was risen! He was alive! He was with them! Without waiting for the morning, they headed back to Jerusalem to share their great good news with the other disciples. Their meeting with the Risen Lord changed everything! Fear and doubt and sorrow evaporated as their hearts grasped the Easter gospel. Jesus lives! And when our hearts truly embrace this great truth, it will transform all our tomorrows!

> Because He lives I can face tomorrow
> Because He lives all fear is gone.
> Because I know He holds the future
> And life is worth the living just because He lives!

43. Charles Wesley – Orpheus To The Christian Church

The legends that come from the Greek Myths is the story of Orpheus. He was so blessed by the gods with the gift of song that nothing on earth, or in the underworld, could withstand the power and influence of his beautiful singing. The story of Orpheus is of course a myth but the Christian Church has a real 'Orpheus.' His name is Charles Wesley. Three hundred and five years ago, in December 1707, Charles Wesley was born and for the last two hundred and fifty years, Christians around the world have been singing the hymns he composed. This 'Orpheus' was the eighteenth child of the Rev Samuel and Susanna Wesley and younger brother of John Wesley. He left home in Epworth, Lincolnshire, in east England, to be a pupil at the very prestigious Westminster School in London. Later he went to study at Christchurch College in Oxford University. There he gathered around him a small number of fellow students who met regularly to pray and study the Bible and devotional books. This was the beginning of the group known later as the 'Holy Club,' and later still as 'Methodists.' So the world's 'first Methodist' was Charles Wesley!

In October 1735 Charles, with his brother John and two friends, sailed for Georgia in America. Charles was employed as Secretary to the Governor of the state and John was minister to the English colonists and missionary to the native Indians. Returning to England a year later, Charles had a very moving experience of personal conversion. It happened on the Sunday morning of May 21st, 1738, which was Pentecost Sunday.

> I arose and looked into the Scripture. The words that first presented were, 'And now, Lord, what is my hope? Truly, my hope is even in thee.' (Ps.39:8)...Again I opened upon Isaiah 40:1, 'Comfort ye, comfort ye, my people, saith our Lord.' ...I now found myself at peace with God and rejoiced in the hope of loving Christ...I saw that by faith I stood; by the continual support of faith, which kept me from falling...I went to bed still sensible of my own weakness ...yet confident of Christ's protection.

Three days later his brother John had a similar conversion in his well-known 'Aldersgate Street' experience. Later that evening, Wednesday, May 24th, John arrived at the house where Charles was recovering from illness, and they sang with some friends a hymn that Charles had just written. That hymn was to be the first of an output of hymns and spiritual songs that would appear non-stop for the next fifty years.

> Where shall my wondering soul begin?
> How shall I all to heaven aspire?
> A slave redeemed from death and sin
> A brand plucked from the fire
> How shall I equal triumphs raise
> Or sing my great Deliverer's praise?

Why are Charles Wesley's hymns still so universally popular? Certainly much more has been written about John Wesley than about Charles, but around the world today Charles is better known and more popularly remembered than John. A simple illustration will prove the point. On any given Sunday in the year, literally tens of thousands of people all over the world will sing Charles Wesley's hymns. These hymns will be sung not only in English but in the scores of languages into which they've been translated. Compared with this worldwide use of Charles's hymns, the number of people who will read one of John Wesley's sermons or theological treatises is very small indeed! So why have Charles Wesley's hymns endured so well for two and a half centuries? In spite of all the new hymns, songs and choruses that continue to be written, why is it that Charles' hymns still have an enduring place in the affection of so many Christians?

The answer to these questions is really quite simple. Charles Wesley filled his hymns with the great doctrines of Scripture. When we sing a Wesley hymn we are singing the truths of the Bible set to music! And that is exactly what Charles Wesley intended. He wrote his hymns so that the Methodist converts would be taught the doctrines of the Bible. Many of the first converts in the Wesleyan Revival in eighteenth-century Britain were illiterate men and women. They could not yet read the Bible for themselves but as they learned the words of Charles' hymns, they were learning Scripture!

Charles wrote many hymns about Christ's first Advent, including the ever-popular:

> Hark! the herald angels sing
> Glory to the new-born King.

In three lines that repeat the word 'born,' he emphasises that Jesus came to be our Saviour.

> *Born* that man no more may die
> *Born* to raise the sons of earth
> *Born* to give them second birth.

Christ's atoning death on the Cross for the sins of the world is a theme in hundreds of his hymns but none has proved more popular than:

> And can it be that I should gain
> An interest in the Saviour's blood?
> Died He for me who caused His pain
> For me who Him to death pursued?
> Amazing love! How can it be
> That Thou, my God, shouldst die for me?

Christ's resurrection is likewise expressed in memorable words in the hymn:

> Christ the Lord is risen today
> Sons of men and angels say ...
>
> Lives again our glorious King
> Where, O death, is now thy sting?
> Once He died our soul to save
> Where's thy victory, boasting grave?

Our ascended Lord is our High Priest who prays for us in heaven. Charles teaches this great doctrine in his hymn:

> Arise, my soul, arise
> Shake off thy guilty fears
> The bleeding sacrifice
> In my behalf appears.
> Before the throne my Surety stands
> My name is written on His hands.

111

The same hymn assures us that we can really know that our sins are forgiven because we have the witness of both the Holy Spirit and the blood of atonement:

> His Spirit answers to the blood
> And tells me I am born of God.

Just as the New Testament proclaims that Christ will come again in power and glory and set up His eternal kingdom, so Charles Wesley echoes 'the glorious hope' in his hymn:

> Lo! He comes with clouds descending
> Once for favoured sinners slain
> Thousand thousand saints attending
> Swell the triumph of His train!
> Hallelujah!
> God appears on earth to reign.

Charles Wesley gave special attention to the doctrine of Scriptural holiness, commonly known by descriptions like 'full salvation,' 'entire sanctification,' 'the second blessing' and 'perfect love.' Among Charles' output of more than eight thousand hymns in total, there are scores and scores of hymns on this doctrine. His understanding of Christian holiness was never better expressed than in his great prayer hymn:

> O for a heart to praise my God
> A heart from sin set free.
> A heart that always feels the blood
> So freely shed for me.

Holiness means that our hearts are cleansed from inner sin and filled with the love of God:

> A heart in every thought renewed
> And full of love divine.
> Perfect, and right, and pure, and good
> A copy, Lord, of Thine.

And God will give this great blessing of a 'clean heart' to His people when He comes in the fullness of His Spirit and imparts His own holy nature to us:

Thy nature, gracious Lord, impart
Come quickly from above.
Write Thy new name upon my heart
Thy new, best name of Love.

We continue to think of Charles Wesley and we thank the Lord for this 'Orpheus of the Church' as we learn Scripture doctrines as we sing his hymns.

44. The Concept Of Perfection

Jesus said, 'You, therefore, must be perfect, as your heavenly Father is perfect' (Matt. 5:48). These words have been examined, argued and debated about in the history of the Church from New Testament times until now. What did Jesus mean by 'perfect'? Surely 'perfection' belongs to life in heaven, not here and now?

Churches that belong to the Wesleyan and holiness traditions have taken these words of our Lord very seriously and tried to understand them in their context. In particular they have noted that this command to be perfect is the conclusion of what Jesus taught in this chapter beginning at v.3. This means that the teaching found in vv. 3-47 must be understood before v.48 can be understood. In this approach they have followed the advice of John Wesley (1703-1791), sometimes called 'the father of the holiness movement.' In his *Explanatory Notes upon the New Testament* (1755) Wesley observed, '[This perfection] refers to all that holiness which is described in the foregoing verses, which our Lord in the beginning of the chapter recommends as happiness, and in the close of it as perfection.' So a study of the earlier verses in Matthew 5 is necessary in order to understand what 'perfect' means in v.48.

Matthew 5:17-20 These verses are a kind of key to the whole passage. Jesus says he has not come to abolish 'the law and the prophets' but to fulfil them. By 'the law and the prophets' he means the teaching of the *Torah*, the first five books of Moses (Genesis – Deuteronomy) and the prophetical books of the Old Testament. The Hebrew word *torah* means 'teaching,' 'instruction,' 'direction,' and while it is used generally of the whole five books of the Pentateuch, it mostly refers to the Ten Commandments that God gave to His people through Moses, recorded in Exodus 20:1-17, and repeated in Deuteronomy 5:6-21. The Ten Commandments were intended by God to teach and guide His people in the way they ought to live. The whole of life was to be governed by these commandments; the first four relate to relationship with God and the other six refer to relationships with one another.

These commandments reflect the character of God who is holy, so when these commandments are kept the result is holy living. Likewise what the prophets taught about how the people should serve God and treat each other is just an application of what the Ten Commandments say. God wants His people to be a holy people and holiness comes by obedience to His laws. Now Jesus says that he has come to enforce this teaching. The holiness enshrined in the Ten Commandments will remain until 'heaven and earth pass away.' Nothing will be taken away from this standard, not even 'an iota or a jot,' meaning, in modern terminology, 'the dotting of the *i* or the crossing of the *t*.' This *Torah* is binding on Christians just as it was binding on Israel in Old Testament times.

Later, in Matthew 22, Jesus says that this whole law is summed up in two commandments. 'You shall love the Lord your God with all your heart ... and your neighbour as yourself' (vv.37-40). Here Jesus is telling us that love is the fulfilment of the law. How do we keep the first four commandments that relate to God? By loving Him with all our heart and soul and mind. How do we observe the six commandments that refer to our duty to our neighbour? By loving our neighbour as we love ourselves. These words of Jesus explain the *Torah* and they explain what holiness is. Holiness is love; loving God and loving our neighbour.

Jesus taught his disciples that their righteousness must 'exceed' the righteousness of 'the scribes and Pharisees' (5:20). The word 'righteousness' is a very important word in both the Old and New Testaments. In the Old Testament it is expressed by the Hebrew word *tsedeq*, meaning what is morally right, what is just; so the Psalmist says that the very heavens declare God's righteousness (50:6). In the New Testament the Greek word for righteousness is *dikaiosune*, which also means what is good and just and right. The words 'righteousness' and 'holiness' are interchangeable; both express the character of God Who is holy and righteous. So in Luke 1 they are used together; we are to serve the Lord 'in holiness and righteousness' all our days (Luke 1:74, 75). When Jesus says that our righteousness must 'exceed' the righteousness of the Pharisees, he is talking about quality, not quantity. In Matthew 23 Jesus is scathing about the 'righteousness' of the scribes and Pharisees. They were concerned with external regulations like paying the tithe but neglecting justice, mercy and faith (v 23). They washed the outside of the drinking cup but ignored the dirt on the inside (v.25). Because of this emphasis on external religion, which neglected true holiness and righteousness of heart, Jesus condemned these religious teachers for appearing to be righteous while really they were 'full of hypocrisy and iniquity' (v.28). By contrast, the 'righteousness' of the Christian exceeds this hypocritical righteousness because it is of the heart and results in holiness; i.e. the love of God and neighbour. This is the 'righteousness' for which we are to hunger and thirst (5:6) and with it we are truly blessed and truly happy.

Matthew 5:43-48   The earlier discussion on verses 17-20 has shown us what 'righteousness' means.   It is a quality of heart; it is the disposition of the soul that directs and empowers the life in holy living. Jesus' teaching can be summed up by saying: a holy and righteous heart is required for holy and righteous living. Now in these later verses Jesus applies this teaching. The true disciple of Jesus not only loves his friends but also loves his enemies (vv.43, 44). Jesus now describes holiness and righteousness in terms of loving; loving God and our neighbour. When we love like that we are reflecting God's great love.   When we 'love our enemies and pray for those who persecute us,' then we are proving that we are the sons of our heavenly Father. God loves like that; He makes the sun to rise and the rain to fall on both good and evil people (v.45). If as Christians we love only those who love us, then, says Jesus, we are no better than the scribes and Pharisees that he condemned so strongly (vv.46, 47).

All through Matthew 5:3-47 Jesus had been teaching, explaining and illustrating what true holiness and righteousness is. It includes the Christ-like character described in the Beatitudes, vv.3-11. This makes the followers of Jesus both salt and light in a sinful world (vv.13-16). The righteousness of his people is in holiness of heart, not empty externals (vv.17-20).   This righteousness, this love of God and

116

neighbour, shuns murder, harsh judgements of others, adultery and seeking divorce in marriage for selfish and sinful reasons (vv.21-32). It also has nothing to do with false testimony and seeking revenge, but instead turns the other cheek, goes the second mile and loves all mankind (vv.21-47).

Having made this teaching clear, Jesus concluded with 'Therefore.' By this he meant a summary, a conclusion, of all this teaching on how his people should live in the world. 'You, therefore, must be perfect, as your heavenly Father is perfect' (v.48). The word 'perfect' here (Greek, *teleios*) means achieving the desired end. In character and conduct God wants His people to be like Him. This 'perfection' is love in action; it is the love of God and neighbour. As John Wesley said, the perfection which Jesus commands in Matthew 5:48 refers 'to all that holiness' described in the earlier verses. In general the Christian Church has always understood perfection in this way and generally this is how it was understood by important Christian theologians like Bishop Augustine (354-430), Martin Luther (1483-1546) and John Calvin (1509-1564). Wesleyan theology, following the teaching of John Wesley, has given particular and emphatic emphasis in understanding perfection in terms of perfected love. The whole teaching of Jesus in Matthew 5:3-47 makes it very plain that perfection is nothing more and nothing less than love in the heart and love in conduct; this is what it means to be 'perfect as your heavenly Father is perfect.'

45. Saint Valentine's Day

Saint Valentine's Day is the annual commemoration held on February 14th, and celebrates affection between young lovers. The day is named after one or more Christian martyrs named Saint Valentine, and was established by Pope Gelasius I in 496AD. It's traditionally a day on which young lovers express their love for each other by presenting flowers, offering confectionery and sending greeting cards, usually anonymously.

The day first became associated with romantics love in the circle of Geoffrey Chaucer in the Highs Middle Agers, when the tradition of courtly love flourished. Numerous early Christian martyrs were named Valentine but the saint honoured on February 14th was Valentine. Valentine of Rome was martyred about 269 and this tradition usually belongs to him.

The first recorded association of Valentine Day with romantic love (1382) is from Geoffrey Chaucer. He wrote, 'For this was Saint Valentine's Day, when every bird cometh there to choose his mate.' This poem was in honour of the first anniversary of the engagement of King Richard II of England to Anne of Bohemia. Valentine Day is referred to by Ophelia in Hamlet (1600-1601).

> To-morrow is St Valentine's day
> All in the morning betime
> And I a maid at your window
> To be your Valentine.

The modern mention of Valentine's Day can be found in a collection of English nursery rhymes (1784).

> The rose is red, the violet's blue
> The honey's sweet, and so are you
> Thou are my love and I am thine
> I drew thee to my Valentine.

Well, there it is! It might be true but in the balance, there are a lot of things that may be added. We just don't know – but we are sure that Christ's love for us is so special! All the Bible tells us that Christ died for us and rose again, and is coming back in glory. What a day that will be! Christ's disciples will be waiting and knowing that it might be soon! Let each of us be strong and faithful, carrying out our business and looking for the King! Maybe it won't happen in our lifetime and when we die, we'll see the Lord in his glory. Dying or living, we shall see the Lord!

46. John Wesley's Bias To The Poor

Beginning with his leadership of the Oxford 'Holy Club,' John Wesley had a deep and sincere care for poor people that marked his ministry for sixty years. Setting up a school for the children of poor families and visiting the prison and the workhouse in Oxford was an expression of how he understood the Christian faith. Long before his contacts with the Moravians in 1735 and his evangelical 'heart-warming' of 1738, John Wesley knew that being a Christian was nothing less than the practice of the Great Commandment of Christ. 'You shall love the Lord your God with all your heart … and your neighbour as yourself.' Loving one's neighbour had a special application to the poor and all those materially and socially disadvantaged.

Wesley continued this ministry to the poor in Georgia and it was given prominence when the United Societies were set up in 1743. The schools opened in Bristol, the Newcastle Orphanage, the free dispensary in London and many other such projects were all the outworking of John Wesley's concern for poor people. In 1759 he wrote: 'If I might choose, I should still, as I have done hitherto, preach the gospel to the poor.' At the age of eighty-two he spent five days walking through the snow on London's streets while he begged and collected £200 for 'the poor of the society.'

While John Wesley was strongly convinced that service to one's neighbour, especially the poor, was a duty laid on every Christian, he was equally convinced that such a life of service is the outcome of genuine Christian experience. Increasingly he described true faith in the words of Paul as 'the faith that works by love.' Through the decades of argument and misunderstanding about his doctrine of Christian perfection, he never retreated from his core conviction about the doctrine; in height and depth it is nothing less and nothing more that the love of God and neighbour. In this way John Wesley's life-long practical care and concern for the poor was a demonstration of that particular understanding of Christian holiness for which he said God had raised up the people called Methodists.

47. The Methodist Pentecost

'Till you press the believers to expect full salvation now, you must not look for any revival.' John Wesley wrote these words in 1766 after observing the work of God in revival. Early in 1760 there was remarkable move of the Spirit among the Methodist people in Otley in West Yorkshire. Although it began in a small way, it was a spark that caused a very large conflagration. The revival was so impressive that John Wesley took time to visit Otley and talk with those caught up in a very significant work of the Holy Spirit. 'In the beginning year 1760 there was a great revival of the work of God in Yorkshire. About thirty persons were met together in Otley in the evening in order to pray, sing hymns, and to provoke one another to love and good works...Thus they continued for the space of two hours, some praising and magnifying God, crying to Him for pardon or purity of heart. Before they parted, three believed God had fulfilled and cleansed them from all unrighteousness.'

John Wesley wrote of Otley that it was 'a glorious work of sanctification' and referred to it as the day of Pentecost. 'Many years ago my brother (Charles) frequently said, "Your day of Pentecost is not fully come, but I doubt not it will. And then you will hear of persons sanctified as frequently as you do now of persons justified." Having carefully observed the Otley revival John Wesley was convinced that Charles' prediction was indeed fulfilled. If John Wesley, always exact and definite in his use of words, likened the work at Otley to that which launched the Church in Jerusalem, then we can be sure it was a revival of great spiritual power. When the history of this Yorkshire move of the Spirit is carefully traced, the undeniable evidence is that whenever the spiritual flame spread, hundreds were converted.

John wrote of Bristol on the September 21st, 1761, 'God was pleased to pour out His Spirit this year on every part of England.' July 24th, 1762, 'I rode to Dublin and found the flame was not only continuing but increasing.' A letter from Limerick in the west of Ireland confirmed that 'a glorious work' was going on there and 'the fire is now spreading on every side.' Wesley returned to England to hear that the fires were burning in many places. From Cheshire came the news that 'there was an outpouring of the Spirit, nor is His hand yet stayed.' In Liverpool he found 'such a work of God as had never been known there before.' Eighteen years after the outbreak of the Methodist Pentecost, John Wesley's judgement on its spiritual impact had not changed. 'The glorious work of sanctification spread from 1760 …and wherever the work of sanctification increased, the whole work of God increased in all its branches.' No wonder Charles Wesley taught the Methodist people to sing:

> See how great a flame aspires
> Kindled by a spark of grace
> Jesu's love the nations fires
> Sets the kingdoms on a blaze.

48. On Fire With God

James Caughey was born in the north of Ireland in 1810. There are very few details of either his exact place of birth or information about his family. He wrote of himself as being of 'Scotch ancestry,' which almost certainly means that his family was Presbyterian. When he was in his mid-teens he emigrated with his family to the United States and by the late 1820s he was working in a flourmill in Troy, New York. About this time he joined the Methodist Episcopal Church and was 'soundly converted to God in Christ.'

Troy was part of what had become known as the 'burned over district' on account of the numerous revivals that had broken out in that area. As Methodism was very much committed to these revivals, it is not surprising that Caughey speaks of how he was caught up in 'a powerful revival of religion,' and from that came his call to the ministry. In the early 1830s he was admitted to the ranks as a preacher on probation and in 1836 he was ordained into the Methodist ministry. He conducted his first revival services in Montreal and Quebec in Canada and some two hundred conversions were recorded and fifty believers were sanctified. These revival services set a pattern that Caughey would follow for the next thirty years of his active, itinerant and revivalist ministry. He saw his congregations made up of three kinds of people who needed specific and pointed preaching to meet their spiritual need. The lost needed to be converted, the backsliders needed to be restored, and, as a convinced Wesleyan, Caughey passionately advocated that all believers needed to be sanctified wholly by the grace of entire sanctification.

Responding to what he believed to be a clear call from God, he set sail for the British Isles and arrived in Liverpool in July 1841. This was to be the first of four visits he made to Britain and they involved him in a growing controversy with the hierarchy of English Methodism. Although he brought to England a certificate from the Troy District confirming that he was a preacher in 'good standing,' he had not been officially invited to Britain either by the Wesleyan Conference or any influential Methodist group. His revivalist services were not welcomed by conservative 'high church' Wesleyans like Jabez Bunting, and Caughey's open attacks on ministers who were not engaged in 'soul-saving' did not endear him to the Wesleyan establishment. For the next six years, Caughey preached in Wesleyan chapels all over the north of England. Everywhere his powerful, pointed and passionate evangelistic preaching resulted in hundreds of open conversions. Caughey preached directly on the great issues of sin, repentance, saving faith, conversion, the realities of heaven and hell, as well as messages directed to Christians who needed to move beyond conversion and be 'sanctified wholly' and enabled to live a life of victory over sin this side of heaven.

In 16 weeks of preaching in five Wesleyan chapels in Sheffield, Caughey's letters recorded that 3266 people had been 'justified' and 1435 had been 'sanctified.' In every service, immediately after the preaching, Caughey encouraged the people to remain for a prayer meeting and it was there that the 'saving work' was done. Caughey moved among the people, urging them to move up to the communion rail as 'penitents' and there they were counselled and prayed for by the local preachers who assisted the evangelist. In this way every penitent was dealt with personally and careful record was kept of the transaction.

He was the first evangelist of note in Britain to make such use of the 'penitent form' and among those who responded in Nottingham was the teenage William Booth, who later modelled his own evangelistic preaching style on the American's. Caughey's habit of keeping numerical records enabled him to give precise details on the numbers who had been justified and sanctified in every service where he preached. At the close of his six-year visit in 1847 he claimed that 20000 sinners had been justified and 9000 Christians had been 'entirely sanctified.' Caughey made three more visits to Britain in the next twenty years and while he never quite recaptured the huge congregations and impressive statistics of his first visit, yet his revival preaching was effective and fruitful. Ill health forced his retirement in 1866 and he died in Highland Park, New Jersey, on January 30th 1891.

In the years between 1848 and his second visit to Britain in 1856, Caughey was in constant demand both in New England and Canada. Caughey published five volumes of *Letters* and his half-dozen books dealt mostly with records of his revival services, his travels in the British Isles and Canada, advice on soul-winning and many hortatory addresses.

49. Two Silver Spoons

Probably the most misquoted text in the whole Bible is 1 Tim. 6:10, which is repeated as, 'Money is the root of all evil'. The full text is, 'The love of money is the root of all (i.e. all kinds) evil.' In that respect John Wesley was clearly saved by grace from any love of money. In the half-century of his evangelistic ministry, he earned thousands of pounds from his publishing enterprises. With his brother Charles, he published no fewer than 400 titles, including letters, journals, sermons, theological treatises, Christian apologetics, biblical commentaries, and much, much else. And he quite literally gave all the money away to poor people and good causes!

Early in the revival he wrote: 'If I leave behind me ten pounds, above my debts and my books, you and all mankind bear witness against me that I lived and died a thief and a robber.' At his death in 1791, his executors found that his total treasury amounted to ten guineas (£10.55)! And his will directed that four of these guineas should pay four unemployed men to carry his coffin and the remainder to be distributed among his poorest preachers.

In one of his sermons he outlined the stewardship of money that he practised all his life. At Oxford he received thirty pounds a year, lived on twenty-eight pounds and gave away two pounds. The next year he received sixty pounds, still lived on twenty-eight and had thirty-two to give away. Years later when he received one hundred and twenty pounds, he continued to live on twenty-eight pounds and was able to give ninety-two pounds to the poor! He once confided in his sister Martha: 'Money never stays with me. It would burn me if it did. I throw it out of my hands as soon as possible, lest it should find a way into my heart.' He gave generously to the poor wherever he met them and was so kind to beggars that his brother Charles once remarked, 'My brother was born for the benefit of knaves.'

In 1776, the Commissioners for Excise were doing an inventory of all the silver plate held privately in England. They were sure that John

Wesley, who had thousands of converts all over the country, must have become rich through all these supporters. They wrote and asked him to declare what quantity of silver plate he owned. His reply was as succinct as it was simple. 'I have two silver spoons at London, and two at Bristol. This is all the plate which I have at present, and I shall not buy any more while so many around me want bread.' John Wesley really believed and practised the counsel of Jesus. 'A man's life does not consist in the abundance of his possessions' (Lk.12:15). At the end of his long and devoted life, John Wesley left behind him just ten guineas – and one hundred thousand converts!

50. When Life Tumbles In, What Then?

This question is prompted by a biblical text and a famous sermon preached in Scotland eighty years ago. The text is Jer. 12:5, 'If thou hast run with the footmen and they have wearied you, then how will thou do in the swelling of Jordan?' The text asks a very simple but important question; if the everyday events of life overwhelm us, how will we cope with life's crises? The 'swelling of the Jordan' means when the river is full and fast and furious, with its raging waters bursting over the banks. Who could cross such a river? So, how will we handle life's great storms? When a loved one suddenly and unexpectedly dies? When the longed-for baby is born with some physical or mental malformation? When a medical report tells us we have an incurable condition? What will we do in that awful hour? Where shall we turn? Will our faith be strong enough? Will God be with us when life tumbles in?

A very moving and helpful illustration comes to us from the ministry of the Rev. Arthur John Gossip (1873-1954). Dr Gossip was a Scottish minister and a very popular preacher. He had been a chaplain to Scottish troops in the First World War, a lecturer in pastoral theology at Trinity College in Glasgow and a parish minister. Week after week his congregation looked forward to Sunday when Dr Gossip would preach morning and evening. He had great gifts in opening, preaching and applying the truths of the Bible. He was also a very dedicated pastor who visited his members diligently and loved being in the homes of his people. In the pulpit or across someone's fireside, Dr. Gossip was pastor, preacher, teacher, counsellor and friend and his people loved him. Then, at the height of his power and popularity, his wife suddenly died. Her death came swiftly and without any warning and Dr Gossip was devastated with grief and sadness. He had visited many a home darkened by death and now the pain of bereavement was under his own roof.

On the first Sunday following his wife's funeral, Dr Gossip decided to preach as usual. The congregation was surprised because they expected their pastor to take some leave of absence as he came to terms with his great loss. In that morning service he led the worship and the Old Testament scripture he selected was Jeremiah 12. He based his sermon on verse 5, asking the question, 'How wilt thou do in the swelling of Jordan?' He entitled the sermon, 'When life tumbles in, what then?' He spoke about the great foundation of faith in the risen Lord Christ. Such a faith does not exempt us from life's crises but it does give us strength and an anchor and hope in the darkest hours. Out of his own recent grief and bereavement the preacher spoke with confidence and deep conviction. The psalmist in ancient Israel knew it; Paul knew it and the saints in every age have known it – God is with us at all seasons and especially when our skies are dark. When our feet slip in the swollen waters of our Jordan, a hand catches us and steadies us; we have a Presence, a Comforter, a Fortifier. He related how some years before he had seen a picture in the National Gallery in London that had moved him very profoundly. It depicts Christ on the Cross in dense darkness and he seems to be alone. But as we gaze into the background we see another form, God's form. We see other hands supporting Christ, God's hands. We see another face, God's face, more full of agony even than our Saviour's own. Gossip's inspiring words gripped his people with their truth and power. 'The presence, the sufficiency, the sympathy of God; these things grow very real and very sure and very wonderful.'

Near the end of the sermon he emphasised the great love of God in Jesus our Lord. 'Our hearts are very frail, and there are places where the road is very steep and very lonely. But we have a wonderful God. As Paul put it, what can separate us from His love?' Not death! Not death! Then in memorable words Dr Gossip gave his testimony and included words from *Pilgrim's Progress*. 'Standing in the roaring of the Jordan, cold to the heart with its dreadful chill, and very conscious of the terror of its rushing, I, too, like Hopeful, can call back to you who one day in your turn will have to cross it, "Be of good cheer, my brother, for I feel the bottom, and it is sound."'

Later, at the request of some members of his congregation, he printed private copies of the sermon. It was handed on from friend to friend and the response was startling. So many people who were experiencing grief and bereavement found the sermon very comforting and reassuring. They identified with Dr Gossip in his personal loss and they wanted to identify with him also in the strong foundation of his faith. After repeated requests from many parts of the world to have the sermon more readily available he consented to its wider publication. In a personal note appended to the sermon he said, 'This sermon has wandered so far over the world, and I have received so pathetically many requests for copies from people in sorrow. I publish it now as it was delivered.'

'What can separate us from the love of God?' and the answer is – nothing and no one! We are safe in the love of God! What confidence! What a glorious certainty! When our faith is anchored in the love and mercy of God revealed in Jesus' death and resurrection, we can face every situation. When the night is dark, when the storm is raging, when all our hopes seem to crash around us – we are kept by the power of God! When life tumbles in, what then? The answer is: The great grace of God outlasts and conquers all our fears, even death itself.

51. John Wesley's War Against Slavery

In 1774, John Wesley published a 53-page tract entitled, *Thoughts upon Slavery*. It was an impassioned argument that slavery is a sin against God; no man should be able to buy and sell another human being. From what he saw of slavery at first hand in Carolina in America in the late 1730s, Wesley was inveterately opposed to it.[1] His conviction that slavery is a sin against our fellow man arose from his understanding of what real Christianity is. To be a Christian is to fulfil our Lord's 'Great Commandment.' 'You shall love the Lord with all your heart ...and your neighbour as yourself' (Matt. 22: 37-40). The love of neighbour can never be reconciled with being a slave owner. Before looking at Wesley's opposition to slavery more closely, a summary of the origins of slavery in the British Empire and the attempts made to end it will be helpful.

From the late 16th century the British Empire had been deeply involved in the slave traffic. Men and women were forcibly taken from Africa and transported to British colonies in America and the West Indies. They were used as slave labour in the tobacco plantations in the New World and on the sugar plantations of the Caribbean. As the empire expanded Britain's plantation owners depended more and more on a steady supply of slave labour. Research has shown that in the two hundred years from 1600 to 1800, no fewer than twelve million black men, women and children were taken by force from Africa and transported as slave labour. This was the largest forced migration of men and women in human history. While these figures are shocking as a catalogue of human traffic, what cannot be computed is the number of slaves who died on the terrible voyages across the oceans. Locked in chains below decks in conditions of unspeakable squalor and often victims of typhoid, dysentery and other diseases, uncounted thousands died at sea and were promptly dumped overboard. The forced labour, the lack of care and medicine for the sick and the harsh regime of the 'killing fields' meant that the mortality rate among the slaves was

---

[1] J Wesley, *Works*, 1:49.

cruelly high. As the slaves died at sea or at work, the slave ships kept up a steady supply of replacements.

An Act of Parliament in 1772 made it illegal to own or employ slaves in Great Britain. Then in March 1807 came the Act that prohibited the transport of slaves on any British ship. This was a landmark achievement in the campaign against slavery. Its success was largely due to the campaigning of William Wilberforce (1759-1833), Member of Parliament and outspoken Christian. He was strongly supported by a number of prominent evangelical Christians, including Thomas Clarkson, Henry Thornton, Granville Sharp and John Venn. These were part of the 'Clapham Sect,' a fellowship of Anglican evangelicals that fought against the slave trade and other injustices and took their name from Holy Trinity Church, Clapham, in London, where they all worshipped. In 1823 a Society was formed for the total Abolition of Slavery. Finally, in August 1833, the British Parliament passed the *Slavery Abolition Act*. It granted freedom to all slaves held in the British Empire.

John Wesley's publication was one of the first important protests against slavery that appeared in England. He began by outlining the rise of slavery in the early 16th century by Spain and Portugal and then by Britain. He refuted the argument that African Negroes were taken from poverty and squalor and transported to better conditions in the West Indies and America. Instead they were treated with the utmost cruelty and contempt. He quoted from the legislation that operated in the state of Virginia that it was lawful to kill any slave who tried to escape. When defenders of slavery argued that the practice was 'authorised by law,' Wesley protested vigorously. 'Notwithstanding ten thousand laws, right is right and wrong is wrong still. Even if we don't consult the Bible, the whole business of slavery is contrary to justice and mercy. But Wesley went further. He boldly defended the Negroes as fellow human beings, made in the image of God as much as white men and women. He was attacking the apartheid practised by the British government of his day that permitted slaves to be treated as chattels because the colour of their skin made them socially and spiritually inferior. Here was John Wesley's doctrine of Christian holiness in action. The love of neighbour could never be reconciled with any form of slavery.

Wesley believed that an appeal to Parliament at this time would accomplish nothing. He was right in this judgement because in spite of repeated attempts by William Wilberforce and his supporters to legislate against slavery, it was thirty-three years after Wesley's publication that Parliament finally prohibited British ships from carrying slaves in 1807. So Wesley directed his tract against the sea captains, the merchants in Glasgow, Liverpool and Bristol who had grown rich on slavery, and the plantation owners. An awful day of retribution is coming. 'O think before you drop into eternity. He shall have judgement without mercy that showed no mercy. The great God will deal with you as you have dealt with them, and require their blood at your hands. And at that day it will be more tolerable for Sodom and Gomorrah than for you.' But John Wesley kept his strongest thunder for the Englishmen who owned plantations in America and were guilty of keeping the vile slave traffic alive. 'You are guilty of fraud, robbery and murder; the blood of all these wretches lies upon your head. The blood of thy brother (for, whether thou wilt believe it or no, such he is in the sight of Him that made him), crieth against thee from the earth... Thy hands, thy bed, thy furniture, thy house, thy lands, are at present stained with blood.'

This was plain speaking indeed! While many of those in high office in Church and state said nothing against slavery, or were even profiting from it, Wesley spoke out prophetically in God's name. Even George Whitefield kept slaves at his orphanage in Georgia in America and defended the practice when he was challenged about it. But John Wesley knew that that the love of God and man could never be reconciled with slavery. Seventeen years later, in 1791, as he lay dying in his house in London, he wrote his last letter. Across more than 60 years of ministry he had written thousands of letters. Now his last letter showed that the old warrior was still thinking about the poor slaves. It was addressed to William Wilberforce who was about to

133

present another anti-slavery petition in Parliament. Wesley encouraged Wilberforce in his 'glorious enterprise in opposing that execrable villainy which is the scandal of religion, of England, and of human nature... O be not weary of well doing! Go on in the name of God, and in the power of His might, till even American slavery (the vilest that ever saw the sun), shall vanish away before it.'

Had John Wesley lived to see the success of Wilberforce's campaign in March 1807 he would certainly have rejoiced. The Law that prohibited British ships from transporting slaves was the first step in opposing the vile trade. Finally, in 1833, the Act was passed that prohibited slavery anywhere in the British Empire. As our nation remembers the Act of 1807, let it not be forgotten that John Wesley's was one of the first voices raised in England. He not only loved God but he also truly loved his brother.

52. Abide With Me

Henry Francis Lyte was born at Edham Roxburghshire, Scotland, on the 1st June, 1793 and throughout his ministry and afterwards, he was known for the hymn, 'Abide with me.' He was sent to Portora Royal School, Enniskillen, Co. Fermanagh, in 1803 and I have heard about him all his life. I attended the near-by Enniskillen School and for the next fifty years I've often thought of Henry Lyte. I have followed the lanes and byways that he uses to know and spent time studying the flora and fauna that he loved. In June 2013, there was a public service held for Lyte at Portora where a plaque was unveiled which read. 'Henry Francis Lyte, 1793 – 1847, Poet and Hymn Writer; Abide with Me; at school 1803 – 1809.' Maybe it's time to write about Henry Francis Lyte!

Lyte went on to Trinity College, Dublin and took orders in the Church of Ireland. He became a curate near Wexford and there he experienced an evangelical conversion after a friend's funeral. In 1817, he became a curate in Marzion, Cornwall, and he met Anne Maxwell, a keen Methodist, whom he married. In 1818 the first son was born and the Lyte's had four other children. A daughter was born but died a month later, and on the April 20th, 1822, another daughter was born and after that two sons; John Walker Maxwell, born on the 2nd January 1825, and Farnhem Maxwell on 10th January 1828.

Lyte took a great delight in poetry and from his time at Portora School, there has been a continuous flow of verse. He published *Tales in Verse illustrative of Several of the Petitions in the Lord's Prayer* (1826), and *Poems chiefly Religious* (1833) and after his death a volume of *Remains* (1850). Three of Lyte's best known hymns are paraphrases of psalms. 'God of mercy, God of Grace' (Ps. 67); 'Pleasant are thy courts above' (Ps. 84); 'Praise, my soul, the King of Heaven' (Ps. 103). Lyte is credited with around ninety hymns and among the most popular are: 'Jesus, I thy cross have taken;' 'Abiding, O so wondrous sweet;' 'Saviour like a shepherd lead us.' He picked up tuberculosis and in 1847 he stood in his pulpit to deliver his farewell message. Referring to our Lord's atoning sacrifice as being a pillow of consolation to the dying soul, he added, 'O brethren, I can speak feeling, experimentally on this latter point; and I stand up here among you seasonably to-day, as alive from the dead.' Lyte and his family went abroad and he died at Nice on the 20th November, 1847 and was buried in the grounds of the Church of England Chapel.

Although Lyte's hymns are sung occasionally, there is one hymn that is sung almost daily, 'Abide with me.' He wrote it during his last illness and has stood for one hundred and seventy years. It is sung the world over and has never lost its popularity. Its popularity grew with the publication of *Hymns Ancient and Modern* in 1861 and the tune 'Eventide,' composed by W.H. Monk, took the public by storm and it has been used ever since. It was the favourite hymn of King George V and VI and was sung at the former's funeral, as indeed at Queen Alexandra's. This hymn was General Gordon's favourite. Edith Cavell sang it as she courageously faced the German firing squad and it was sung at Kitchener's Memorial Service in 1916. Frederick Wall, then Secretary of the Football Association in 1927, looked at the programme and saw it was to be the band playing 'Alexander's Rag-Time Band.' He wrote this out and substituted Lyte's 'Abide with me.' He handed the message to King George V who was present, and the King stood and bared his head. This was the Wembley Cup Final and it has been used ever since. Dr Ian Bradley considered this hymn indelibly imprinted upon the Victorian mind and he called it, *'Abide with Me; The World of Victorian Hymns,'* in his scholarly 1995 edition of hymns.

The whole tone of the hymn points immediately to an approaching death. Phrases like 'Swift to its close ebbs out life's little day,' 'Hold thou Thy cross before my closing eyes,' and 'Heavens morning breaks and earth's vain shadows flee,' probably points to Lyte's own death.

> Abide with me! Fast falls the Eventide
> The darkness deepens, Lord, with me abide
> When other helpers fail, and comforts flee
> Help of the helpless, O abide with me!

Lyte knew the tuberculosis had a hold upon him and he composed his hymn for loved ones, friends and companions as they felt led to seek God. The eventide was coming, the darkness deepens other helpers could not save him and he turned to the Lord. 'Help of the helpless, O abide with me.'

Swift to its close ebbs out life's little day
Earth joys grow dim, its glories pass away
Change and decay in all around I see
O Thou who changest not, abide with me.

However long is life it will eventually pass away and Lyte sees all life dying as he is. The glories vanish, all of life stops and 'earth joys grow dim, its glories pass away.' The familiar, the fading families, old friends - all of life changes and decays but the Lord of eternity is with him. 'O Thou who changest not, abide with me.'

Not a brief glance I beg, a passing word
But as thou dwellest with thy disciples, Lord
Familiar, condescending, patient, free
Come, not to sojourn, but abide with me.

The glorious Lord was with his people and that lasted until eternity. No shadow of fear could drive Lyte away and with him eternal life will be their lasting possession. Familiar! Condescending! Patience! Free! Oh what words are these! 'Come, not to sojourn but abide with me.'

The eight verses of this hymn are full of glorious words that shine through the dying man. 'O Thou who changest not;' 'Familiar, condescending, patient, free;' 'Through cloud and sunshine;' 'I fear no foe;' 'I triumph still;'

'Point me to the skies,' and the triumphant lines that runs through the hymn nine times, 'Abide with me.' The last verse points to a beginning that has no end - life with Christ will be for ever.

Hold thou thy cross before my closing eyes
Speak through the gloom and point me to the skies
Heaven's morning breaks and earths vain shadows flee
In life, in death, O Lord, abide with me.

Henry Lyte ended his days in triumph. As we follow his lines in the hymn, let us make sure that we will reign and live with Him for ever.

53. A Tercentenary Tribute to
Charles Wesley, 1707-2007

Charles Wesley, born 300 years ago this year, is the most prolific hymn-writer in the history of the Church. He wrote about 8500 poetical pieces, most of which were hymns based on the doctrines of the Bible. This immense output represented approximately 180,000 lines of poetry, making him the most productive writer of verse in English. This is considerably more lines of poetry than that which came from the pens of William Shakespeare, or John Milton, or William Wordsworth. Most of his most popular hymns have been translated into almost every language where the Christian gospel is known. On any given Sunday, in Christian congregations around the world where traditional hymns are still sung, more of Charles Wesley's hymns will be sung than those of any other Christian poet. So this tercentenary year of Charles' birth is an appropriate time to look in some detail at his life and work and especially his hymns.

The origins of the Wesley family can be traced back almost to the Norman Conquest but accurate history begins with Charles' great-grandfather, the Revd Bartholomew Westley (an early spelling of the name) (c.1596-1671). He was vicar of Charmouth in Dorset, and his son John Westley, an Oxford graduate, became minister of the parish church in Winterbourne Whitchurch, Dorset, in 1658. These were politically troubled days in England as Oliver Cromwell's republic came to an end, followed by the Restoration of the monarchy in 1660. The Royalist government of King Charles II was openly hostile to all things Puritan and in the next few years the laws enacted in the Clarendon Code were aimed at punishing all those of decided Protestant and Reformed convictions. The 1662 Act of Uniformity required that all Church services be conducted only by the use of the Prayer Book, now revised in an openly anti-Puritan way. Some 2000 of England's parish ministers refused to sign the Act, representing about one fifth of all the clergy. Heavy penalties were imposed on these 'Dissenters.' They were removed from their parishes and many were fined or imprisoned or both. Both Bartholomew Westley and his son John were among the protestors and they were driven from their parishes. John's son, Samuel, was born in 1662, the year of the expulsions. He studied at Oxford, joined the Church of England which had expelled his father and grandfather, and was ordained in 1689. He married Susanna Annesley, daughter of the very prominent Puritan dissenter, Samuel Annesley, who had also been expelled in 1662. The Revd. Samuel Wesley had a brief curacy in London, and later moved to be rector of South Ormsby in Lincolnshire in 1691. In 1696 Samuel became rector of Epworth in north Lincolnshire. The 'Wesley Story' really begins then and today the name 'Epworth' is known throughout the Christian world because of the Wesley association.

At least 17 children were born to Samuel and Susanna and ten survived beyond infancy, three sons and seven daughters. Charles was born on 18th December 1707. It was a remarkable household in which the Wesley children were brought up and its spirituality left a lasting impression on Charles. In his Epworth rectory home the two great streams of 17th century English Church tradition met and coalesced, Anglicanism and Puritanism. From his parents Charles Wesley imbibed the love of tradition, the Book of Common Prayer and the importance of regular communion – all Anglican emphases. But he also inherited the Puritan tradition; the love of learning and good books, the providence of God in everyday life, the unbroken link with the Protestant Reformation, and the conviction that this life is a serious and disciplined preparation for the life to come. Charles' father Samuel, and his oldest brother, Samuel Junior (1690-1749) were both able poets and from them he learned much about the art of verse and metre and rhyme. Their mother Susanna taught all the children, and school began on the day of the child's fifth birthday. Susanna taught by repeating a particular lesson until the child had grasped it thoroughly. When Samuel asked her on one occasion why she had persisted in repeating a particular lesson twenty times, her reply was simple. 'If I had given up after nineteen attempts, it would have been lost labour for me and the child.' The Christian faith, the doctrines of the Church of England, and the place of prayer, devotion and scripture reading in the Christian life, were all attended to with great seriousness in the Wesley household. Such was the pattern of the regular, systematic and structured Christian life-style taught and practised by Samuel and Susanna Wesley that it could be claimed that Epworth was truly 'the cradle of Methodism' and not just biologically!

A few months after his eighth birthday Charles Wesley went from his mother's 'kitchen school' in Epworth to Westminster School in London. For the next ten years he laid an excellent educational foundation, especially in the Classics. He excelled in the study and translation of Latin and Greek. For the rest of his life he understood and practised the careful metrical exactness he found in the poetry of Ovid, Horace, Virgil and Homer. In 1726 he was elected to Christchurch College, Oxford. At Oxford he had been preceded by his great-grandfather Bartholomew, his grandfather John, his father Samuel and his two older brothers, Samuel Jun. and John. Four successive generations of the Wesley family preached the Christian gospel and Charles would make his own distinctive contribution to that unique family record.

Early in 1729 Charles began to meet regularly with three or four of his undergraduate friends. They read the Bible together and other devotional books. John Wesley joined the group in November 1729 and because he was the oldest, and already ordained a minister in the Church of England, he became its leader. Their regular attendance at prayer and Holy Communion earned them jesting epithets; the 'Holy Club,' 'Bible Moths,' 'Enthusiasts.' Then came the nickname that would stick – 'Methodists,' a description of their methodical and disciplined living. While John Wesley is almost always credited with being the founder of Methodism, in fact his brother Charles was the first 'Methodist.' It was Charles who organised the first small group of Oxford 'Methodists,' which John later joined. Charles graduated MA in March 1733 and in September 1735 he was ordained deacon and then priest in the Established Church.

Later that year Charles and John, with two friends, sailed for Georgia, a British colony in America. John was a missionary with the Society

141

for the Propagation of the Gospel (founded in 1701) and Charles was personal secretary to the newly appointed Governor of Georgia, General James Oglethorpe. Charles' time in Georgia was marked by unhappiness, a sense of spiritual failure and he was plagued with ill health. Five months after his arrival, he left the colony and returned to England. Having met Moravian Christians on the voyage to America, he now made friends with these German evangelical believers in London and through their spiritual guidance, he and his brother John found the experience that was to change their lives and make them evangelists. On Pentecost Sunday, May 21st, 1738, Charles Wesley, in his own words, 'found peace with God' – as John did three days later. The evangelical conversions of the Wesley brothers was the spark that lit the great spiritual fires of England's 18th century Evangelical Awakening.

During his years at Oxford Charles Wesley had experimented with writing poetry but the 'heart-warming' of Sunday, May 21st, 1738, made him England's greatest scripture poet. The following day he began to compose a hymn that explained his conversion. Out of a full and rejoicing heart he penned what has always been labelled his 'Conversion Hymn.' The first of the seven verses reads:

> Where shall my wondering soul begin
> How shall I all to heaven aspire?
> A slave redeemed from death and sin
> A brand plucked from eternal fire.
> How shall I equal triumphs raise
> Or sing my great Deliverer's praise?

The former self-confessed 'Pharisee' had become a humble believer in Christ the Lord! The Oxford Methodist had become an evangelical Methodist! The seeker had become a finder! Charles longed to tell the good news of the gospel to others and with his brother John, he itinerated in England, Wales and Ireland. For the next seventeen years he travelled far and wide on horseback, preaching the gospel and establishing the new 'Methodist Societies.' These 'Societies' would become the Wesleyan Methodist denomination of the 19th century, the forerunner of world Methodism. There are many eyewitness accounts of Charles' preaching ministry. Whether his congregation was in a church, or a field, at a crossroads or on a hillside, the people heard him gladly. With the cloth workers in West Yorkshire, the coal miners in Co. Durham, the farmers in Ireland or the tin miners in Cornwall, the common people to whom he preached loved him.

It was, however, his vast output of hymns that was to give Charles Wesley enduring fame. From the 'Conversion Hymn,' written in May 1738, until his final verses, composed shortly before his death in March 1788, Charles wrote some 8500 poetical pieces. His average composition was some ten lines of poetry every day, of every week, of every month, of every year, for fifty years! With very few exceptions, his poetry was lyrical. He turned Biblical doctrines into hymns that expressed both scripture truth and (often) his own Christian experience. His poetry always has both rhyme and rhythm and he has given us scores of hymns that are among the most familiar to all who sing the great classical English hymns. We need only mention some examples. 'O for a thousand tongues;' 'Jesus, lover of my soul;' 'Love Divine, all loves excelling;' 'Christ the Lord is risen today;' 'And can it be?;' 'Rejoice, the Lord is King;' 'Hark, the herald-angels sing.'

54. There's More With Us Than With Them

We all need encouragement in these days as we live our lives and serve the Lord. There's more with us than with them!! (2 Kings 6:11-19). We begin the New Year with a Bible event from 2 Kings and an anecdote from Birmingham. For a number of years the king of Syria had tried to capture the prophet Elisha. Elisha always knew what the Syrians were planning and revealed their plans before they could be carried out. Finally the Syrian armies surrounded Elisha in Dothan. When Gehazi, Elisha's servant, woke up and saw the encircling Syrian armies, he was terrified. Elisha prayed, 'Lord, open his eyes.' When Gehazi looked again, he could hardly believe what he saw. All round them were horses and chariots of fire. The armies of heaven were protecting them! And Elisha encouraged him. 'Don't fear, there's more with us than with them!' Immediately the Syrians were struck with blindness and Elisha and Gehazi escaped.

Often we need to ask the Lord to open our eyes. When our strength has failed and faith is weak, we're apt to think that God has forgotten us. But He hasn't! He is near and only our dimness of vision prevents us from seeing His great presence and power and provision. Fear not! Trust God! Believe His word! There's more with us than with our enemy!

In the early 1950s a well-known department store in Birmingham, England, wanted to extend its premises. Close at hand was an ideal site but it belonged to the Quakers whose Meeting House had been there for well over two hundred years. The department store wrote to the Quakers, offering to buy the site. They said, 'We will give you a very good price for the land. In fact, we'll send you a blank cheque. Please fill in whatever sum of money you think appropriate and we will honour it.' Four weeks passed and there was no reply, then five weeks, then six weeks. Finally a letter arrived from the Quakers. It thanked the department store for their generous offer but declined to accept it. 'Our Meeting House has been here for almost two hundred and fifty years,' they explained, 'much longer than your store. We have no wish to sell our property. However, if you would agree to sell your site to us, we are very interested in buying it. We will give you a very good price for it. Just state your selling price and we will honour it.' The letter was signed 'Cadburys.' The department store thought they were dealing with a small congregation of Quakers. Instead they were dealing with the Cadburys' empire. Cadburys could have bought the department store twenty times over!

When our enemy the devil attacks us, by ourselves we are weak and feeble. But when Christ dwells in us by His Spirit, we are mighty! The devil is no longer attacking us; he is attacking the Captain of our salvation – and the devil cannot win! There's more with us than with him! As we go through 2006, be encouraged. With Christ we are more than conquerors!

55. John Wesley's Doctrine Of Responsible Grace

The Revd John Wesley (1703-1791) was the founder of the Methodist Societies in Britain in the 18th century. From that 'Methodist' revival have sprung all the Methodist Churches around the world. In 19th century America the Holiness Movement developed from the 1830s and from that Movement there emerged Holiness Churches, like the Free Methodist Church, the Wesleyan Church and the Church of the Nazarene. All these Methodist and Holiness Churches hold Wesleyan doctrines, meaning the doctrines of the Christian faith found in John Wesley's writings. He reacted strongly against the high Calvinist doctrines of unconditional election and limited atonement. The former meant that out of all humanity, God had elected to save only some and all the rest were damned. The latter meant that when Christ died to make atonement for the sins of the world, he died only for those whom God had elected.

In response to these Calvinist doctrines which he believed to be unscriptural, John Wesley set out his 'order of salvation' as his scheme is often called. Wesley strongly argued that God's love for sinners is universal; He loved not just some lost men and women (the so-called 'elect') but he loved the whole world of human beings (John 3:16). When Christ 'died for our sins' (1 Cor. 15:3) He died for the sins of the whole world. John Wesley proclaimed a gospel that all men and women *could* be saved, if they respond to God's grace.

When we come to look carefully at John Wesley's doctrine of salvation (known as *soteriology*) we see immediately that its foundation is the universal love of God. Another name for God's love is grace, so grace becomes the key to Wesley's teaching. He believed that from the creation of mankind in the Garden of Eden until the final consummation of all things at the end of the world, all God's dealings with men and women are through His grace. So he wrote, 'All the blessings which God hath bestowed upon man are of his mere grace, bounty or favour: his free, undeserved favour, favour altogether undeserved.'

John Wesley's doctrine of salvation begins with what he called 'preventing' or 'prevenient' grace. This is the grace of God that 'prevents' or 'goes before' our response to Him. Without God's grace we are, in Paul's words, 'dead in transgressions and sins' (Eph. 2:1). Of our own will we cannot come to God, we cannot respond to God and we cannot break the power of sin in our hearts. Thus we are hopelessly lost – were it not for God's great grace. By His Holy Spirit, God graciously works in our hearts to give us spiritual understanding, to awaken us to our need of God's forgiveness, and to enable us to say 'Yes' when He calls us to repentance and faith in Christ. So our salvation begins with God's grace, and that grace precedes, it 'goes before,' any response that we make. If we respond to this *prevenient* grace, then God's gives us *convincing* grace, the grace by which we know that we must be saved. Then *prevenient* grace and *convincing* grace is followed by *converting* grace. This means that if we repent of our sins and believe in Jesus Christ as our Saviour and Lord, we are born again into God's family. At every step on this journey, from the moment of our first spiritual awakening until we have the witness of the Holy Spirit that we are children of God (Rom. 8:16), it is God's grace that enlightens us, enables us to repent of our sins and strengthens our will to believe in Christ for salvation.

Prevenient grace, of itself, is not salvation; we must respond to this grace. God's grace leads us, as we might say, from grace to grace, and so Paul says, 'By grace you have been saved, through faith' (Eph.2 8). John Wesley summed up his doctrine of salvation by faith like this. Without God's grace we *cannot* be saved; without our response of repentance and faith, enabled by grace, God *will not* save us. So we are responsible before God; we can either accept His grace and love and be saved, or we can reject His mercy and be lost. Today many Wesleyan theologians speak about John Wesley's doctrine of *responsible grace*. God loves us, Christ died for us, the Holy Spirit awakens and draws us toward Christ but we are responsible for the choice we make – either faith or unbelief.

John Wesley believed that this doctrine of responsible grace is found throughout the Bible. In Ezek. 18:1-4, God says clearly that each human person is responsible before Him for their actions. The children are not punished for the sins of their fathers (v.2); rather 'every living soul' (v.3) is responsible before God. It is the man or woman who continues to sin against God, who will not accept the offer of God's love and forgiveness, who will 'die' (v.4). Here, 'die' does not refer to physical death but to eternal separation from God.

If the wicked man 'turns away from all the sins he has committed' (v.21), he shall not be condemned. This passage presupposes that the wicked man can make a responsible choice; he can either continue in his sin or turn to what is 'just and right.' God takes no pleasure in punishing the wicked; rather He wants all men and women to be saved (v.23). Our responsibility before God is further emphasised in vv.24-29. The righteous man may choose to turn away from righteousness and go back to old sinful ways. If he does, his former righteousness will not save him. John Wesley's understanding of responsible grace is the foundation of Wesleyan theology. God's grace makes the salvation of all people possible; it also makes every man and woman responsible for their actions, including their response to God, of either faith or unbelief.

56. The Hymns Of John Newton

John Newton, converted slave-trade captain and Anglican minister, is best known as the author of the hymn, 'Amazing grace! How sweet the sound.' The familiar lines:

> That saved a wretch like me
> Twas grace that taught my heart to fear
> Tis grace has brought me safe thus far
> And grace will lead me home.

These were all written out of Newton's own life-transforming experience of Christ's saving grace. In the many other hymns that came from his pen, the most dominant themes were Christ as Saviour and Lord, the wonder of saving grace, regeneration by the Holy Spirit, the certainty of sins forgiven and the promise of eternal life. Unlike the hymns of his contemporary, Charles Wesley, most of which can be dated almost to the year, it is difficult to date Newton's hymns with any certainty. His 'Amazing grace ...' was written sometime between his taking up a civil service job in Liverpool in 1755 and the publication of *Olney Hymns* in 1779.

In all, Newton wrote some three hundred hymns and about twenty of them are still in use today. Practically all his hymns were inspired by his study of the Scriptures. This is true even of the two hymns that are certainly autobiographical. The theme of 'Amazing grace' comes from King David's reaction to the Lord's promise to him that his son and successor on the throne of Israel would build the Lord's House. 'Who am I, O Lord God, and what is my house, that you have brought me thus far?' (1 Chron. 17:16). Likewise his hymn, 'In evil long I took delight' reflects the Gospels' accounts of Christ's death and Newton sub-titled it, 'Looking at the cross.' It was Newton's meditation on the Song of Solomon that inspired the hymn that was to be second only to 'Amazing grace' in popular appeal. When he read 'Thy name is as ointment poured forth' (Songs 1:3), he thought of One whose name was far more significant and more enduring than Solomon's or any other human name.

> How sweet the name of Jesus sounds
> In a believer's ear.

Newton entitled the hymn 'The Name of Jesus' and the verses are a believing and devotional commentary on who Jesus is and what he has done. For two centuries this hymn has been sung by those, who like Newton, have seen in the name 'Jesus' a summary of all his attributes and graces and glories. For the believer that Name 'soothes his sorrows, heals his wounds, and drives away his fears.' It is 'manna to the hungry soul' and to the weary it is 'rest.' That lovely Name is our foundation, our defence against the Devil's attacks and our inexhaustible supply of God's unfailing mercies.

> Dear name! The rock on which I build
> My shield and hiding place
> My never-failing treasury filled
> With boundless stores of grace.

Then in lines that thrill with love and devotion and worship, Newton inspires us to sing the biblical descriptions of our wonderful Lord!

> Jesus! my Shepherd, Husband, Friend
> My Prophet, Priest, and King
> My Lord, my Life, my Way, my End
> Accept the praise I bring.

The one-time blasphemer was now a new man 'in Christ' and he looked forward to that great Day when he would see his Lord and praise him in the New Jerusalem. For Newton and for all Christians, the time between now and then should be filled with our service and witness to His dear name.

> Till then I would thy love proclaim
> With every fleeting breath
> And may the music of thy name
> Refresh my soul in death.

Newton's exaltation of Christ a Saviour, Lord and Friend was well expressed in another hymn.

> One there is above all others
> Well deserves the name of friend
> His is love beyond a brother's
> Costly, free, and knows no end.

This hymn was suggested by Proverbs 18:24, 'There is a friend that sticketh closer than a brother.' As in so many of his hymns, Newton emphasises Christ's atonement. He never forgot that 'the One hanging on a tree' was dying there for sinners.

> Which of all our friends to save us
> Could or would have shed their blood?
> But our Jesus died to save us
> Reconciled, in him to God.

As a very diligent pastor, John Newton encouraged his people to be a part of the fellowship of their church and to use all the means of grace. He urged them, in the words of Scripture, 'Not forsaking the assembling of ourselves together' (Hebrews 10:25). Hearing the word of God preached and sharing in prayer are essential disciplines for growth in grace.

> Great Shepherd of thy people, hear
> Thy presence now display
> As thou hast given a place for prayer
> So give us hearts to pray.

The hymn goes on to speak of the 'holy peace' found in God's house, where 'love and concord dwell,' where the troubled conscience can find relief and where wounded spirits can be healed. So the pastor prays for his people and for himself.

> May we in faith receive thy word
> In faith present our prayers
> And in the presence of our Lord
> Unburden all our cares.

In his sermons Newton spoke of how he was often attacked with unbelief. Did he really trust God? Could he trust God? As he pastored his people he learned that other Christians often felt the same way. Based on the words of Isaiah 12:2, 'I will trust and not be afraid,' he wrote a hymn to express a confidence in God's love and providence – a confidence to conquer every doubt.

> Begone unbelief
> My Saviour is near
> And for my relief

Will surely appear.
By prayer let me wrestle
And he will perform
With Christ in the vessel
I smile at the storm.

The references to 'storm' and 'vessel' were echoes of his days as a sailor on the high seas and particularly the wild night of March 21st, 1748 that was a turning point in his life. Although it was not a full conversion experience, his escape from near death silenced his atheism and from that night he never swore or blasphemed again. Later in the hymn he speaks of how God was watching over him while he was 'Satan's blind slave' and while he 'sported with death.' God's mercies are sure and we can trust his love in every circumstance.

His love in time past
Forbids me to think
He'll leave me at last
In trouble to sink.
Each sweet Ebenezer
I have in review
Confirms his good pleasure
To help me quite thro.'

The many references to prayer in John Newton's writings testify to the importance of prayer in his own life and how he encouraged others to pray. One of his hymns on prayer has long been a favourite with Christians in many denominations.

Come, my soul, thy suit prepare
Jesus loves to answer prayer
He himself has bid thee pray
Therefore will not say thee nay.

Newton remembered the words of Jesus when He taught 'that men ought always to pray and not to faint' (Luke 18:1). The Bible is full of passages that assure us of God's good will for his people. 'Let us therefore come boldly unto the throne of grace, that we may obtain mercy, and find grace to help in time of need' (Hebrews 4:16).

Thou art coming to a King
Large petitions with thee bring
For his grace and power are such
None can ever ask too much.

It was on this theme of prayer that John Newton wrote one of his most moving and encouraging hymns. Every line burns with the author's conviction that we are never more blessed than when we come to God in prayer. After nearly two hundred years this glorious hymn has lost none of its power to inspire us to pray.

Approach, my soul, the mercy-seat
Where Jesus answers prayer
There humbly fall before his feet
For none can perish there.

Thy promise is my only plea
With this I venture nigh
Thou callest burdened souls to thee
And such, O Lord, am I.

When doubts and fears fill our hearts and when the Devil and the powers of darkness bear down upon us, we should run to God in prayer. Then John Newton has a precious verse that is surely among the very best he ever wrote. In four wonderful lines that we should inscribe on our hearts, he reminds us that He who died for us will never forsake us. Our Crucified and risen, ascended Lord is also our Refuge and our Strength.

Be thou my shield and hiding place!
That, sheltered near thy side
I may my fierce accuser face
And tell him, 'Thou hast died.'

We've looked at just some of the hymns of John Newton, the former slave-trader turned pastor and poet. His hymns resonate with the conviction of a man who had really proved God. Newton is not just a good poet; his poetry is nothing less than a commentary on passages of Scripture. He believed, he loved, he studied, he treasured and he preached the Bible as the Word of God. In this bicentenary year of his death, we recall, with praise and thanks to God, John Newton's transformed life and the hymns he has passed on to succeeding generations. Our final example is a hymn based on Psalm 87:3, 'Glorious things are spoken of thee, O city of God.' Zion is the city of God and only God's 'Amazing grace' can make us citizens of that city and its privileges are for time and eternity.

> Glorious things of thee are spoken
> Zion, city of our God! ...
>
> Saviour, if of Zion's city
> I thro' grace a member am
> Let the world deride or pity
> I will glory in thy name.
> Fading is the worldling's pleasure
> All his boasted pomp and show
> Solid joys and lasting treasure
> None but Zion's children know.

57. Justification By Faith:
The Heart Of John Wesley's Preaching

'If any doctrine within the whole compass of Christianity may be properly termed fundamental, they are doubtless these – the doctrine of justification and that of the new birth.' John Wesley wrote this in the year 1746 and throughout his life he never varied from it. Looking back on the years of revival, he admitted that from May 24th, 1738, wherever he was desired to preach, 'salvation by faith was my only theme.' Clearly Wesley wanted it to be known that an important new emphasis entered his preaching in May 1738. He confessed that before that time he did not 'know' salvation by faith, which, in its context, means that he did not understand the doctrine of faith. This admission is surprising, given Wesley's devotion to the teaching of the Church of England, for Article 11 states, 'We are accounted righteous before God only for the merit of our Lord and Saviour Jesus Christ …wherefore that we are justified by faith only is a most wholesome doctrine.'

This reference made Wesley in the year 1738 was not a cast-off remark. Twenty years later he wrote, 'I think on justification just as I have done any time these seven and twenty years.' In a letter to the Countess of Huntington in 1771 Wesley declared that 'for above thirty years' he has preached, 'we are saved from sin, we are made holy by Christ.' The plain, scriptural notion is pardon, the forgiveness of sins. His sins in thought, word and deed are covered. God will not afflict on the sinner what he deserved to suffer. 'The son of his love has suffered for him. And from that time …he loves and blesses and watches over us for good, even as if we had never sinned.'

In his *Journal* he used a variety of expressions in describing his evangelical preaching. 'I there offered Christ… I offered the grace of God….I offered the redemption that is in Christ Jesus… I proclaimed Christ crucified…. I proclaimed free salvation…. I declared the free grace of God…. I exhorted the wicked to forsake his way…. I began to call sinners to repentance…. I invited all guilty, helpless sinners.' Near the end of his life, when, in his own words, he 'was on the borders of the grave,' he confessed: 'About fifty years ago I had a clearer view than before of justification by faith. In this, from that very hour, I never varied, no, not an hair's breadth... By the grace of God I still witness the same confession, By this grace ye are saved through faith.' No wonder that the Lord used John Wesley throughout his long life.

58. Loved With Everlasting Love

(Jer. 31:3). One of the greatest and most comforting doctrines taught in the Bible is the love of God for His people. It is found in almost every book in the Bible, both Old Testament and New Testament. In the Law and in the Prophets; in the poetical and historical books; in Gospels and Letters – all agree to tell us what God said to His people through Jeremiah. 'I have loved you with an everlasting love' (31:3). It was that love that moved the Father to send His Son into the world (John 3:16). Paul writes glowingly of 'that great love with which He loved us' (Eph. 2:4). John emphasises the same great truth in a magnificent creed of just three words: 'God is love' (1 John 4:8). Quite simply there is nothing in all creation more reassuring, more comforting, more encouraging, more uplifting than to know that God loves us. And we can go further and put it in personal terms as Paul did. 'He loved *me* and gave himself for *me*' (Gal. 2:21).

How can we illustrate the illimitable love of God? Of course the greatest depiction of that love is Christ dying for us on the cross. Can we find an everyday illustration, an event or a true story, that will light up this great doctrine for us? One such illustration comes from the life and ministry of John Wilbur Chapman. Chapman was born in Richmond, Indiana, in June 1859, ordained into the Presbyterian ministry and pastored a number of churches. In 1893 he went into full-time evangelistic ministry. He was joined by the famous song leader Charles Alexander and in a ministry that foreshadowed Billy Graham and Beverly Shea, Chapman and Alexander evangelised around the world until Chapman's death in 1918.

Chapman used many memorable personal illustrations in his preaching. In one of them he told of how one evening he was travelling by train in a rural part of the state of Kansas. The only other passenger in the carriage was a young man and Chapman noticed that he was becoming very agitated. He kept glancing out of the window and then covering his face with his hands. Chapman asked if he could help. The young man was a bit reluctant but finally opened up. Many years before he had run away from home and 'sown his wild oats.' He had not contacted his parents for many years and now he was afraid they wouldn't want him back. He had written home some weeks before and told them he would be travelling on this train. At a certain point it passed very close to his home. In the letter he had begged his parents' forgiveness and asked if they wanted him to come home. If so, they were to tie a yellow ribbon on the old apple tree that grew right beside the railway lines. 'Sir,' he said to Chapman, 'the train will soon pass my home but I'm afraid to look. If there's a yellow ribbon on the tree, I'll get off at the next station and go home. If there's no ribbon, I'll just travel on. But I'm too afraid to look out for the tree.'

Chapman offered to look for him. The young man hid his eyes and Chapman kept watch. 'You can open your eyes now,' he said a few minutes later. The returning prodigal looked at Chapman with tears and quivering lips. 'All is well,' said the evangelist. 'There is a yellow ribbon on the apple tree. In fact, there's far more than one. Every branch is hanging with yellow ribbons, scores and scores of them. Your parents love you so much and want you to come home.' If parents can love their wayward children like that, how much greater is the love of God! Truly, we are loved with everlasting love.

59. On His Father's Tombstone

This year, 2003, is the tercentenary of John Wesley's birth. Most of the celebrations planned for this occasion are taking place in this month of June, because Wesley was born on June 28th, 1703. These celebrations are not confined to Britain but are taking place across the world where Wesley's 'Methodism' is part of the Christian Church. Because he was born in Lincolnshire, a highlight of the celebrations will be a service in Lincoln Cathedral on Sunday, June 29th. But John Wesley was not born in Lincoln; rather in the (then) small town of Epworth, some forty miles northwest of Lincoln. In his rectory home were instilled those principles of devotion, discipline, hard work and learning that were to be the trademarks of later 'Methodism.' In a very real sense this Epworth rectory home was the cradle of 'Methodism' – and not just biologically!

Yet Church history might never have heard of John Wesley or Methodism because a fire that gutted his home in February 1709, when he was a child of five, almost claimed his life. The rest of the family escaped safely, only to discover that 'Jacky', as the family called him, had been forgotten in the panic. Then the family saw his frightened face at the attic window of the fire-engulfed house. His father Samuel tried to go up the stairs but he could not pass through the raging flames. Two men ran forward, one stood on the shoulders of the other and lifted the child out of the flames only minutes before the entire roof and front wall collapsed. His mother Susannah was convinced that God has saved their son from the fire for His own purposes. Years later, at the height of his ministry, an artist painted a picture of John Wesley, with a burning house in the background. Underneath, as a caption, were the words of Zechariah, 'Is not this a brand plucked out of the fire?' (3:2).

John Wesley made his first preaching visit to Epworth in June 1742. He had not been there for seven years, since the time of his father's funeral. As an ordained minister in the Church of England, he asked the Curate if he might assist him on the Sunday morning, either in reading prayers or preaching. But the Curate, knowing of Wesley's itinerant ministry, had no intention of having a 'rebel' preacher in his pulpit. Following the service, Wesley's travelling assistant, John Taylor, stood at the church gate and announced: 'Mr Wesley, not being permitted to preach in the church, designs to preach here at six o'clock.' The news spread like wildfire! 'Old parson Wesley's son be back and he be preaching in the churchyard!' The whole area was packed with people as the be-gowned Oxford don and open-air revivalist took his stand on his father's flat tombstone. While the church authorities could forbid John Wesley from preaching in the pulpit or the graveyard, they could not prevent his standing on his father's grave, for it was Wesley family property.

What a scene it must have been! Merchant and miller, farmer and fisherman, soldier and smithy, weaver and washerwoman – all were there in that large, gaping crowd. How many of them remembered the preacher as a small, pensive child taking his place every Sunday in the family pew? Were there some among them who remembered the rectory fire thirty-three years before – perhaps even those two brave, unknown men, who rescued England's future evangelist from the flames? Now John Wesley stands on his father's tomb on that Sunday, June 6th, 1742, and as the evening shadows begin to fall across the 13th century St Andrew's Church, he proclaims his text. 'The kingdom of God is… righteousness and peace and joy in the Holy Ghost' (Rom. 14:17).

John Wesley stayed for a week on that first visit home to Epworth. Every morning he preached at the town cross and every evening from his father's tomb. He visited many homes in the parish where he had been his father's curate and scores of men and women came to faith in Christ as a result of that visit, and the many more visits he made to Epworth in the coming years. Later he reflected on his earlier curacy and his present itinerant ministry, and wrote. 'I am well assured that I did more good to my parishioners in Lincolnshire by preaching three days on my father's tomb than I did by preaching three years in his pulpit.' John Wesley certainly didn't despise parish ministry but he had learned that preaching out-of-doors reached many people who did not attend church services.

And so, with all the Wesley tercentenary celebrations this month, all Christians, and especially those of us who live in Britain, have reason to thank God for His servant, John Wesley. From Epworth in Lincolnshire, there arose a river of grace in 18th century England that, like Ezekiel's, flowed out to bless and heal the land. Or, to change the metaphor, at Epworth was the first kindling of that holy conflagration that would soon, in the words of Charles Wesley, 'Set the kingdoms on a blaze.'

60. Be Still And Know That I Am God

'This is the house of God …this is the gate of heaven' (Gen. 28:17). This old story tells us that God often meets us in the most unexpected places. The words were spoken by Jacob and he was not one of the more attractive people we meet in the Bible. His very name means 'cheat' or 'supplanter.' He had deceived his old blind father, Isaac, and had stolen his brother Esau's family birthright. And then he ran away; away from home, away from his family, away from God – or so he thought. With only a stone for a pillow and the bleak desert around him, he lay down to sleep and had a dream. In the dream to saw a ladder that reached to heaven, with angels going up and down the ladder. These were God's messengers of communication. The God of Scripture is a speaking God and He is always trying to get our attention. Often, like Jacob, we're too tired, or too busy, or too self-occupied, to hear the Lord's voice. Jacob woke from sleep, thought about the dream – and knew what it meant. God is here! He's here with me in this empty desert! His angel messengers are around me! This is God's house! This is the gate of heaven!

And that's just the point. Wherever we are just now that place can be for us the gate of heaven. When we're in church we expect to feel the presence of God. But our Lord is not restricted to church buildings. He comes to us where we are. Often, as with Jacob, He comes uninvited. There is no mention in the Genesis story that Jacob prayed, or wanted God or even thought about Him. God comes seeking us before we seek Him. The English poet Francis Thompson wrote of how he tried to run away from God. 'I fled Him down the nights and down the days; I fled Him down the arches of the years.' But he could not escape from 'those strong Feet that followed, followed, after.' In this poem, *The Hound of Heaven*, Thompson is describing his conversion. The God he fled from found him and Thompson found himself in God's house. It was the same with Jacob. His name was later changed from Jacob to 'Israel,' meaning a prince with God. Who knows what great things can happen to us when we find ourselves in the house of God …at the gate of heaven!

61. Learning To Pray By Example

Luke 11:1: 'Lord, teach us to pray.' Luke tells us that the disciples asked Jesus to teach them how to pray after he had just prayed. This is very important. In his preaching Jesus had spoken about prayer; e.g. Matt. 6:5-8. He had also included prayer in his teaching; e.g. Luke 18:1. But it was neither his preaching nor teaching on prayer that inspired this request from his disciples; it was his example in prayer. Also Jesus had sent his disciples out to preach, yet their request was not, 'Lord, teach us to preach.' They had witnessed the mighty miracles that he performed and saw the astonishment of the crowds (Luke 9:43), but they did not ask him, 'Lord, teach us to perform miracles.' No, they asked instead, 'Lord, teach us to pray.'

The disciples were beginning to learn that there was a direct link between the prayer life of Jesus and his Spirit-anointed ministry. We need go no further than what we find here in Luke's Gospel to see the consistent prayer life of Jesus. As news of his mighty ministry spread far and wide, 'great multitudes gathered to hear and be healed' (Lk. 5:15). This was 'high noon' in the ministry of our Lord and as the crowds gathered to hear him, 'he withdrew to the wilderness and prayed' (v.16). The next chapter tells us that Jesus made a habit of having whole nights of prayer. 'In those days he went out into the hills to pray, and he continued all night' (6:12). A little later the evangelist records that immediately following the feeding of the five thousand, the disciples were with Jesus – and he was praying (9:18). When Luke recounts the Transfiguration of Jesus, he says the Lord took Peter, John and James up the mountain 'to pray' (9:28).

Luke wants his readers to know about the prayer life of Jesus. At every step of his ministry we see Jesus praying. He prayed early in the morning before the day began; he prayed late in the evening after hours of demanding ministry; he prayed in secret; he prayed with his disciples, and he often prayed all night. He prayed in homes; he prayed by the roadside; he prayed on mountains; he prayed in boats; he prayed in the wilderness; he prayed in the synagogue; he prayed in the Garden of Gethsemane; he prayed on the Cross.

No wonder that Jesus' example in praying prompted his disciples to ask, 'Lord, teach us to pray.' As we read and study the life and ministry of our Lord, we will be likewise moved to ask him, 'Lord, teach *us* to pray.

62. Where Love And Justice Meet

From the beginning of his ministry, the prophet Jeremiah knew he would not be popular. He had been called by God to preach in the closing years of the kingdom of Judah. His ministry began in about 626BC and he lived to see his homeland overrun by the Babylonian armies and Jerusalem sacked and burned in 587BC. When God first called Jeremiah, he was left in no doubt as to what was going to happen. The kingdoms of the north would invade all the cities of Judah and Jerusalem itself because the people had forsaken the Lord and worshipped pagan gods (Jer. 1:14-16). God had determined judgement on His people because of their sins, yet that was not the whole story. Judgement was coming but it could be averted. God had planned punishment but there was a way of escape.

Jeremiah was commanded by the Lord to go to the potter's house and watch what the potter did (18:1-2). He saw the potter shaping a clay jar and as he watched, the jar crumbled and fell apart. Instead of throwing the clay aside, the potter began to rework the clay and made from it a new vessel. Then Jeremiah heard the Lord's word. "O house of Israel, can I not do with you as this potter has done?" (v.5). Then Jeremiah knew that he was watching a parable being enacted. Just as the potter had patience with the broken clay, so God was patient with his people. If they continued in their sin and disobedience, God's judgement would fall – but there was always the possibility of repentance.

This message of hope is made clear as God speaks further to Jeremiah. If God determines judgement on a nation, that means it will be plucked up, broken down and destroyed (18:7). Such judgement is God's response to our sin and wickedness and our refusal to mend our ways. In the earlier chapters of the book of Jeremiah there are records of many warnings that he gave to the people of Judah and Jerusalem. Speaking in God's name he warned his people that they had exchanged the God of their fathers for false gods (2:10-13). He pleaded with them to turn back to the Lord who was gracious and who would not be angry forever (3:11.12). Using a familiar farming illustration he reminded them that the harvest was past, the summer had ended and the nation was in great danger (8:20).

Now in the potter's house God again repeats His intended judgements – but adds a wonderful word of hope. If the nation against whom He has planned disaster will "turn from its evil," then God will "repent" of His threatened judgements (18:7,8). This is Jeremiah's 'Gospel of Hope.' In the gathering darkness a light still shines. If Judah and Jerusalem will "repent" God will visit them, not in judgement but in blessing. Their repentance will avert the divine punishment. Repentance is not just a change of mind, not just merely being sorry that our sins have found us out. It means a sorrow for sin that leads to a forsaking of sin; a turning away from wrong doing and seeking the Lord in deep contrition.

The Lord spelled out very clearly what His offer of salvation was. He was "shaping evil" against His people and "devising a plan" to destroy them (18:11). What did that mean? How can a holy God "devise evil"? How could God destroy His own people? Had He not promised to protect and deliver them from their enemies? Was there not a covenant, an agreement, between Israel and her Lord? There was but it was not an unconditional covenant. The conditions were that if Israel obeyed the Lord and served Him faithfully, He would protect them (Jer. 11:1-8). But Israel had not kept her promise. They have forgotten me, the Lord says, and are offering worship to pagan gods (18:15). So He is planning "evil" against them to punish their disobedience. The Hebrew word translated 'evil' is *ra'ah*. It doesn't mean that God is lashing out in anger against His people. It means rather that He is responding as a holy God to their continued sinfulness. God is always gracious and loving and merciful but He is also just and cannot let sin go unpunished. When He says that He will repent, it doesn't mean He has done wrong and is now sorry for it. It means that when a nation turns back to Him in genuine sorrow for their sin, He will rescind the just judgement He had planned.

166

This passage teaches us a lot both about the character of God and the response that nations and individuals can make to Him. God's justice and holiness means He cannot tolerate sin. He must punish sin or else He is not a holy God. But His judgement against sin is not so fixed and predestined that He cannot do other than punish. This whole episode of what Jeremiah saw and heard in the potter's house is full of reminders that people and nations can repent of their sin and turn to God. Yes, God has planned judgement against sin but He has equally planned mercy for those who turn from sin.

Now Jeremiah understands why he was told to go to the potter's house. He saw an earthen vessel "spoiled" although the potter tried to make something good of it. God was like the potter. For centuries He had cared and loved and protected His people, but in spite of all He had done for them, they turned away from Him. They were like the "spoiled" clay in the potter's hand. But now the great drama of salvation and hope began to take shape. Instead of discarding the "spoiled" clay and choosing new clay in its place, the potter began to rework the old clay. If Israel will turn back to the Lord and let herself be as clay in His hands, He will remake her and save her and deliver her from the otherwise inevitable judgement.

Jeremiah's 'Gospel of Hope' is a reminder that the Lord always wants men and women and nations to turn to Him. He offered a way of escape to the doomed city of Sodom (Gen. 18:23-32). He sent the prophet Jonah to warn the people of Ninevah (Jon. 4: 9-11). He preached through the prophet Ezekiel that He has no pleasure in the death of the wicked but rather wants him to turn back from his wickedness and live (Ezek. 33:11). He declared through the words of Isaiah that He "waits to be gracious [and] to show mercy" (Is. 30:18).

Jeremiah's message offered a gracious salvation to his nation – but they wanted none of it. Even after he had explained both the terrible prospect of judgement and God's offer of mercy, the people refused to change their ways. They spurned the divine love and ignored the grace God offered. "We will follow our own plans and will every one act according to the stubbornness of his evil heart" (Jer. 18:12). Jeremiah's sermon on grace and the terrible events that followed remind us forcibly that if men and nations refuse the divine mercy they will suffer the divine judgements.

63. The Prayer For Mercy And Grace

Hebrews 4:16. 'Let us then with confidence draw near to the throne of grace that we may receive mercy and find grace to help in time of need.' It is appropriate that this series on the prayers of the Bible should finish with this prayer. It is a prayer for mercy and grace and we are <u>always</u> in need of both! Throughout this letter to the Hebrew Christians, there are many invitations and encouragements to pray. In this passage we are exhorted to 'come boldly' and we also have, 'we draw near to God' (7:19); 'those who draw near to God' (7:25); 'the way into the holiest' (9:8); 'the new and living way' (10:20); 'let us draw near' (10:22); 'whoever would draw near to God' (11:6). We should study each of these expressions carefully for they all emphasise what glorious privileges we have to come into the presence of God.

This prayer in chapter 4 begins with great encouragement. We are to come to God 'with confidence.' All through the Bible we have the Lord seeking His people and wanting fellowship with them. God really wants us to come to Him with our praises and our prayers! The reason for this confidence is given in v.14. The ascended Lord Jesus is our 'great High Priest' who has gone into heaven on our behalf. He sympathises 'with our weaknesses' for He too was tested and tempted but remained sinless (v.15). Because Jesus is praying for us, we have confidence to come to God in prayer.

When we do 'draw near' to God in worship, praise and prayer, we receive mercy and grace. What a promise is this! We are always in need of mercy for we are constantly tempted, and, as Jeremiah said, were it not for the Lord's mercies, we would be consumed (Lam. 3:22). As the day begins we need to come to God to seek his face and ask his mercies for what lies ahead. Who knows what news the post will bring today? What situations we will find ourselves in? What dangers await us? What temptations we will face? What lies around the corner for ourselves and those we love? Yes, we need the Lord's mercies and he invites us to come to him.

But that is not all. The verse also promises that when we draw near to God he gives us grace. Grace! What a word it is! It is truly one of the great words of the Bible! Who can define grace? Who can describe grace? Who can explain grace? It means God's gracious and all-sufficient provision for all our needs. When God promises to give us grace, he is promising to give us his love, his forgiveness, his healing, his presence, his tender compassion. Amazing grace indeed! And God promises it to us today, and tomorrow and every day of our pilgrimage! So let us every day 'draw near to God' in prayer.

64. John Wesley's Theology

The Revd John Wesley (1703-1791) was the leader of the spiritual awakening in 18th century Britain, known as the Methodist Revival. Born in Epworth, some 150 miles north of London in Lincolnshire, he went to Charterhouse School in London and later to Christ Church, Oxford University. There, with his brother Charles, he became the leader of a spiritual movement in the university, the members of which were derisively called the 'Holy Club' or 'Methodists.' Following two years of disappointing ministry in Savanna, Georgia, he returned to England. There, on May 24th, 1738, he experienced his evangelical 'heart-warming,' and the next year he began half a century of itinerant evangelism. His converts and followers were known as 'Methodists' and the movement spread from Britain to America in the 1760s. John Wesley's teaching was called 'Wesleyanism' and in this article we will be looking at John Wesley's theology. What did he believe and teach about God and mankind and salvation?

We begin with *the love of God*. Of all the doctrines found in Wesley's writings, the doctrine of God's love is the most prominent. He believed passionately that the God of the Bible, the creator of the world, is a God of love. In all his preaching he stressed the great truth of John 3:16, 'For God so loved the world that he gave his only begotten Son...' Certainly Wesley believed that all men and women are sinful, that we have all sinned and that we are under condemnation. But for John Wesley that was only half the truth! We are sinners – but we are *loved* sinners! God does not love our sin but he loves us. Indeed He loves us so much that he sent His Son, Jesus Christ, to be the Saviour of the whole world. In particular John Wesley was very opposed to any doctrine that limited God's love. He strongly preached and wrote against the teaching that God loves only some men and women – the so-called elect. For fifty years he preached God's universal love. All men and women everywhere can be saved, because God loved them and Christ died for them. This theology was the foundation of his great ministry. Wherever he preached, he told men and women that they not only needed to be saved but they could be saved. There are no barriers to the love of God. Wherever in the world we live, regardless of the colour of our skin, the language we speak, or our social status, God loves us in His Son who died for us. When John Wesley was dying in London in March 1791 he made one last request of his friends. He asked them to print and give away copies of his sermon, *The Love of God*. The request was carried out and ten thousand copies of the sermon were given away free. In the hour of his death, as in all the years of his ministry, John Wesley was still preaching the love of God.

John Wesley's theology also emphasised *salvation by faith*. This is the good news of the gospel. We can be saved from our sins through faith in Christ. By 'salvation' John Wesley meant the whole process by which, from being sinners, we become the children of God. It works like this. Through hearing the gospel, usually by preaching, we are convicted by the Holy Spirit that we are sinners. But the gospel also shows us that Christ died for us and that salvation is by faith in Him. The Spirit enables us to turn away from sin, that is repentance, and believe in Jesus as our Saviour and Lord. Of the thousands of sermons that John Wesley preached, mostly in the open-air, two of his favourite texts were, 'Believe in the Lord Jesus Christ and thou shalt be saved' (Acts 16:31), and, 'By grace ye are saved through faith' (Eph. 2:8). Quite simply, Wesley believed that salvation by faith *is* the Christian gospel and all his work and ministry for fifty years was concerned with proclaiming this fundamental truth. Theologians often use the term *soteriology* which means the doctrine of salvation. In this connection it can be said that John Wesley's theology was first and foremost soteriological. Once in a letter to his brother Charles he wrote: 'You and I have nothing to do but save souls.' By that he meant that proclaiming the doctrine of salvation by faith was their primary task as preachers. This doctrine of salvation by faith does not mean that God does everything and that we have nothing to do with our own salvation. Only God's grace can save us but God does not force that grace upon us. When John Wesley preached salvation by faith, he argued, and explained and encouraged men and women to respond to the gospel's invitation. God gives sinners the grace by which they hear the gospel,

172

by which they understand the gospel and by which they are enabled (but not forced) to believe in Christ. This doctrine of salvation by faith treats us as responsible men and women. We can respond to God grace and be saved – but equally we can ignore or refuse his grace and thus bring about our own judgement and condemnation.

John Wesley's theology included the doctrine of *the witness of the Spirit*. By this he meant that it is the privilege of every born-again believer to know for sure that his sins are forgiven. The scripture he used most often in preaching this doctrine was Romans 8:16, 'The same Spirit beareth witness with our spirits, that we are the children of God.' Wesley emphasised that there are two parts to this witness of the Spirit. There is first the inner assurance in our own hearts that God has forgiven our sin, adopted us into his family and given us eternal life. Then there is the outer witness, that is, the evidence of a life being transformed by God's grace. The Christian loves God and his neighbour and begins to live a life that manifests the fruit of the Spirit. Early in the work of the Revival Wesley thought that this witness of the Spirit comes to every Christian at the very moment of their conversion. After some years however, he was convinced that for some Christians, the inner witness comes days, weeks or even months after their conversion. But he never ceased to preach and write that if the Spirit's witness does not come immediately, it certainly *will* come and the Christian must pray for it, believe for it and expect it every moment. John Wesley knew that this doctrine of the witness of the Spirit brings great joy and peace and assurance to the Christian's heart. The doctrine is found in many of Charles Wesley's hymns. A good example of this is the hymn beginning, 'Arise, my soul, arise.' Two lines in one of the stanzas assure us:

> The Spirit answers to the blood
> And tells me I am born of God.

John Wesley's theology especially emphasised the *doctrine of entire sanctification*. Whereas justification is the pardon and forgiveness of our *sins*, entire sanctification is the cleansing away of our inner *sin*. Wesley said that while justification is God doing something *for* us (restoring us to a new relationship with him), entire sanctification is

God doing something *in* us – taking away the love of sin out of our hearts. He called this doctrine by a number of names, including 'Christian perfection,' 'full salvation,' 'perfect love,' 'Christian holiness' and 'the second blessing.' He believed that God had raised up the Methodist preachers to proclaim this doctrine of 'scriptural holiness' all over the land. As the work of the revival developed, John Wesley formed 'Societies' where the converts met together for fellowship, prayer and instruction from the Bible. In these 'Class Meetings' and 'Band Meetings,' the Methodists were encouraged to seek the blessing of entire sanctification by faith.

Increasingly, John Wesley preached entire sanctification in terms of what the Bible calls 'perfect love' (1 John 4:18). The Holy Spirit is the sanctifying Spirit and God's love is 'shed abroad in our hearts by the Holy Ghost' (Rom. 5:5). Wesley taught that we grow in God's grace from the moment we are saved and this growth is what the Scriptures call sanctification. By the grace of sanctification we grow in love to God and our neighbour and the power of sin is daily being weakened in our hearts. But there is more, John Wesley taught, because God wants all His people to experience *full* or *entire* sanctification. This is the fullness of God's love in our hearts and this is what Jesus meant by the 'Great Commandment,' in Matthew 22:37-39, 'Thou shalt love the Lord thy God with all thy heart... all thy soul... all thy mind... Thou shalt love thy neighbour as thyself.' In the heart filled with love to God and neighbour, said John Wesley, there is no room for pride, or jealousy, or self-will, or resentment, or love of the world or any other manifestation of sin. By faith we can experience this full sanctification now. But John Wesley also taught something else about this entire sanctification that is very important. The fully sanctified Christian must continue to grow in love and holiness. The way of holiness is not a *cul-de-sac*, a kind of spiritual dead end; instead it is a highway, leading onwards and upwards to heaven itself.

Of course John Wesley's theology contained more than these four doctrines. He had a doctrine of creation, a doctrine of the Church, a doctrine of the sacraments and a doctrine of the end of the world, among others. But these four; on the love of God, justification by faith, the witness of the Spirit and entire sanctification, were what he called 'the grand fundamental doctrines' of real Christianity.

65. Know Your Disease! Know Your Cure!

In the *Journal* of the Revd John Wesley (1703-1791), founder and leader of the Methodist Societies, there is an unexpected and interesting hiatus for the eight-week period of December 1756 and January 1757. Since the beginning of his 'field preaching' in Bristol in April 1739, Wesley had been fully occupied with itinerant evangelism and almost every week found him traveling the roads of Britain and Ireland in his non-stop gospel ministry. Now, however, in late 1756, he took an unexpected break and used the time to write a theological treatise. Entitled *The Doctrine of Original Sin according to Scripture, Reason and Experience*, it ran to 522 octavo pages and was Wesley's single longest publication. It was intended as a page by page rebuttal of a book published 17 years earlier by Dr John Taylor of Norwich, *The Scripture Doctrine of Original Sin Proposed to Free and Candid Examination*. Wesley confessed that he had waited some time in the hope that others would reply to Taylor. When this did not happen, he took up his pen because he could no longer be silent. 'Necessity is laid upon me to provide those who desire to know the truth with some antidote against that deadly poison which has been diffusing itself for several years through our nation, our Church and even our Universities.'

John Wesley was deeply disturbed and concerned about the spread of Socinianism in England and its corollary denial of the doctrine of original sin. Named after the Italian rationalists, Lelio Sozzini (1525-1562) and Fausto Sozzini (1539-1604), Socinianism advocated a reductionist Christology and an Enlightenment repudiation of the traditional doctrine of original sin. Wesley's concern was both doctrinal and practical; theologically he viewed Socinianism as destructive of the very foundations of the Christian doctrines of incarnation and redemption, and evangelistically he saw it as a very real threat to the proclamation of the gospel and the work of bringing men and women to Christ.

John Wesley's interest in the doctrine of human sinfulness had begun much earlier than his encounter with John Taylor's book in the 1750s. In 1725, as he prepared for ordination in the Church of England, he carefully examined the *Thirty-Nine Articles* so that he could swear his allegiance to them without quibble or reserve. In particular he had studied Article IX, entitled 'Of Original or Birth-Sin,' and in subsequent years he would quote from it approvingly as an expression of Scripture doctrine.

> Original Sin standeth not in the following of Adam (as the Pelagians do vainly talk), but it is the fault and corruption of the Nature of every man, that naturally is engendered of the offspring of Adam; whereby man is very far gone from original righteousness, and is of his own nature inclined to evil ...and therefore in every person born into this world, it deserveth God's wrath and damnation.

Two weeks after his ordination in September 1725, Wesley preached his first sermon at Fleet Marston. The sermon was entitled 'Death and Deliverance,' based on the words of Job, 'There the wicked cease from troubling ...' (3:17). In the opening paragraph the twenty-two year old preacher reminded his listeners that the miseries of life hardly needed proof. 'The words of Job, "few and evil have been the days of the years of thy servant," may be justly applied to the whole race of mankind. Such is the inheritance which the sin of our first father has entailed on his whole posterity.'

Five years later John Wesley preached two sermons in November 1730 that indicate his ongoing concern with universal sinfulness. The first, entitled, 'The Promise of Understanding,' was preached in All Saints, Oxford, and the second, 'The Image of God,' two weeks later in St Mary's, Oxford. The importance of this latter sermon is that it was his first 'university sermon.' The leader of the Oxford 'Methodists' took for his text the words of Genesis 1:27, 'God created man in his own image.' The sermon gives a vivid description of Adam before and after the 'Fall,' and both sermons enlarge on man's sin and ignorance and spiritual declension. While neither sermon deals directly with the subject of Adam's sin corrupting the human race, the whole argument presupposes the Fall in a very orthodox way, as summarised in Article IX of the *Articles*.

Later, in 1730, in correspondence with his father Samuel Wesley, John Wesley wrote about his concerns over a recently-published book dealing with original sin. In 1729 Archbishop William King published *An Essay on the Origin of Evil* and John reported to his father his deep dissatisfaction with King's doctrine. King argued that evil arises from matter as all creation must be inferior to the Creator. Wesley dismissed King's thesis as a revival of Stoic thinking and pointed out that King made no use of Genesis 3 nor did he account for fallen humanity as in Article IX of the *Articles*. It is very clear that from 1725, the year of his ordination, John Wesley was deeply concerned about how the doctrine of original sin was being marginalized even by Anglican theologians. Well before his evangelical 'heart-warming' in May 1738, Wesley was already convinced of a doctrine of original sin as summarised in Article IX of the *Articles*. When he convened the first Conference of 'Methodist' preachers in 1744, it was significant that they engaged in a discussion on the doctrine of original sin. The consensus arrived at in 1744 represented the understanding of human sinfulness that John Wesley firmly held and defended for the rest of his life.

> Question. In what sense is Adam's sin imputed to all mankind?
> Answer. In Adam all die; that is, (i) Our bodies then became mortal. (2) Our souls died; that is, were disunited from God. And hence, (3) We are all born with a sinful, devilish nature. By reason whereof, (4) We are children of wrath, liable to death eternal. (Romans 5:18; Eph. 2:3).

Ten years after John Wesley began his itinerant preaching ministry across the British Isles, he encountered Socinianism first-hand. In his *Journal* for Sunday, August 28th, 1748, he recorded a preaching visit to Shackerley in Lancashire.

> Abundance of people were gathered before six, many of whom were disciples of Dr. Taylor's, laughing at original sin and, consequently, at the whole frame of scriptural Christianity. Oh, what a providence it is which has brought us here also among

178

these silver-tongued Antichrists. Surely a few, at least, will recover out of the snare and know Jesus Christ as their wisdom and righteousness.

Three years later he was back in Shackerley and recorded: 'Being now in the very midst of Mr Taylor's disciples, I enlarged much more than I am accustomed to do on the doctrine of original sin, and determined, if God should give me a few years life, publicly to answer his new gospel.' Two more examples of Wesley's fear of the destructive influences of Dr John Taylor's doctrine can be cited. Preaching in Belfast on April 6th, 1769, Wesley related: 'I stood in the street and strongly declared, "All have sinned and are come short of the glory of God." But this many of them had no ears to hear, being faithful followers of Dr. Taylor.' But even more pointed was a paragraph in a letter from Wesley to Augustus Toplady in December 1758. 'I verily believe no single person since Mahomet has given such a wound to Christianity as Dr. Taylor. They are his books, chiefly that upon original sin, which have poisoned so many of the clergy and indeed the fountains themselves - the universities in England, Scotland, Holland and Germany.'

Who was this John Taylor whose teaching John Wesley opposed so vehemently? Taylor (1694-1761) was born at Lancaster and spent the greater part of his life as a Nonconformist minister in Norwich where he built the famous Octagon Chapel in 1756. An ardent disciple of the anti-Trinitarian Samuel Clarke (1675-1729), he steadily moved to a Socinian position and in 1740 he published, *The Scripture Doctrine of Original Sin Proposed to Free and Candid Examination*. In 1757 he was appointed to teach theology at Warrington Academy, a stronghold of Socinianism and not far from Shackerley where Wesley had confronted Taylor's disciples in 1748. Taylor's book had been hugely influential and in 1758 Jonathan Edwards lamented the harm it had done in New England. It was this work from the pen of Taylor that Wesley set himself the task of answering in December 1756. His *Doctrine of Original Sin*, together with a later summary sermon, *Original Sin*, sets out his teaching.

Opening his treatise, Wesley quickly came to the point. He could no longer remain silent 'against that deadly poison which has been diffusing itself for several years through our nation, our Church and even our Universities.' He judged Taylor's book more dangerous than 'open Deism;' indeed it is 'old Deism in a new dress,' sapping the foundation of 'all revealed religion, whether Jewish or Christian.' Framing an overall view of human history from Genesis 3 to the present, he painted a stark and realistic picture of fallen man through the ages, dealing, in turn, with the Israelites, the Romans, the Heathen, the Mahometans and, finally, the whole Christian world, both Protestant and Roman Catholic. Everywhere and in every age Wesley found evidence of human pride, malice, envy, hatred, fear, lying, treachery and murder. 'Universal misery is at once a consequence and a proof of this universal corruption. Men are unhappy because they are unholy.'

How can we account for universal human wickedness? Wesley's answer was to quote from Genesis 3, 1 Cor. 15:22, and Romans 5:12. 'In Adam all die,' by the first man came both natural and spiritual death, by 'this one man sin entered into the world ... and death passed upon all men in that all have sinned.' John Taylor had argued that it was unjust of God to punish others because of Adam's sin. The only consequence of Adam's sin that affected the human race was physical death. Wesley replied that since Adam's posterity was punished with death therefore all men were justly punishable. By 'punishment' Wesley said he meant 'suffering consequent upon sin. All mankind suffer death consequent upon Adam's sin... Adam sinned, his posterity suffer and that in consequence of his sin.' Along lines similar to the arguments for original sin found in the writings of Augustine, Luther and Calvin, Wesley saw Adam as the federal head of the race. In the 'Fall' of Adam, all men and women are represented.

> In and through their first parents all Adam's posterity died in a spiritual sense and they remain wholly 'dead in trespasses and sins' till the second Adam makes them alive. By this one man sin entered into the world and passed upon all men. And through the infection which they derive from him, all men, are, and ever were, by nature entirely alienated from the life of God, without hope, without God in the world.

John Taylor asserted that it was inconsistent with the teaching of scripture to say that because of Adam's sin all of us have been put in the hands of the devil. Surely God, in all his dispensations, has been working to deliver us from the devil? Wesley read Taylor's argument as a specimen of Enlightenment optimism about human nature that ignored the plain teaching of Scripture. 'What can be made clear from the scriptures is this: That from Adam sin passed upon all men, that hereby all men, being by nature dead in sin, cannot of themselves resist the devil and that, consequently, all who will not accept help from God are taken captive by Satan at his will.'

John Wesley was convinced that Taylor's rejection of the doctrine of original sin held by the Christian Church from New Testament times resulted in his corollary rejection of the biblical doctrines of grace. Taylor described the new birth and regeneration as merely 'the gaining those habits of virtue which make us children of God.' Wesley expostulated that if that is what regeneration is, then Paul should not have written, 'You are all the children of God by faith in Christ Jesus' (Gal. 3:26), but 'You are all the children of God by gaining habits of virtue.' Wesley's doctrine of regeneration was built on the foundation of universal sin and regeneration is a radical transformation of our fallenness by God's almighty grace.

> According to the whole tenor of scripture the being born again does really signify the being inwardly changed by the almighty operation of the Spirit of God; changed from sin to holiness, renewed in the image of Him who created us. And why must we be so changed? Because without holiness no man shall see the Lord, and because without this change, all our endeavours after holiness are ineffectual.

Two years after his *Doctrine of Original Sin* was published, Wesley wrote a personal letter to Taylor. His style was polite and courteous but he pulled no punches when he described the chasm between their respective doctrines.

> It is Christianity or heathenism! for, take away the scriptural doctrine of Redemption or Justification and, that of the New Birth, the beginning of sanctification, or (which amounts to the

181

same) explain them as you do, suitable to your doctrine of Original Sin, and what is Christianity better than heathenism? wherein, save in rectifying some of our notions, has the religion of St. Paul any pre-eminence over that of Socrates or Epictetus? Either I or you mistake the whole of Christianity from the beginning to the end! Either my scheme or yours is as contrary to the scriptural as the Koran is. Is it mine, or yours? Yours has gone through all England and made numerous converts. I attack it from end to end. Let all England judge whether it can be defended or not!

In taking time to refute John Taylor's book, John Wesley was attempting to answer one of the most erudite and popular Socinian publications of the eighteenth century. His knowledge of Scripture and his ability with the biblical languages are well demonstrated in these pages, nor is there any less evidence of his close acquaintance with the classics, the Church Fathers and the English Puritans. But the real reason for Wesley's long reply to Taylor was his conviction that Taylor's denial of the doctrine of original sin threatened the whole gospel message. He warned against this danger in his 1759 sermon, *Original Sin.*

All who deny this, call it original sin, or by any other title, are but Heathens still in the fundamental point which differences Heathenism from Christianity...Is man by nature filled with all manner of evil? Is he void of all good? Is he wholly fallen? Is his soul totally corrupted? Allow this and you are so far a Christian. Deny it and you are but a Heathen still...O beware of all those teachers of lies who would palm this upon you for Christianity. Keep to the plain, old faith, 'once delivered to the saints,' and delivered by the Spirit of God to our hearts. Know your disease! Know your cure! You were born in sin: Therefore 'ye must be born again,' born of God.

66. Praying With The Prayers Of The Bible

Num.11:10-15. 'Moses said to the Lord, I am not able to carry all this people alone, the burden is too heavy for me...' Moses prayed this prayer in a day of dark depression and discouragement. The opening verses of the chapter relate how divine punishment fell on the people of Israel because they complained about almost everything. Moses prayed and the punishment stopped but not the people's complaints. They wanted meat to eat. For years they had been sustained by manna from heaven but now they longed for the fish, cucumbers and melons they had eaten in Egypt (vv.5,6). They forget how the Lord had delivered them from Pharaoh's bondage. Now the preferred Egyptian food, and the slavery that went with it, to the goodness of the Lord and His provision for them. Moses was beside himself with despair. Would these ungrateful people never stop complaining? Then the Lord's anger threatened the people again (v.10).

Moses was caught in the middle. On one side of him the people complained and on the other side God's wrath was about to fall. He couldn't go on. His frustration broke out in petulant questions to the Lord. 'Why are you dealing so severely with me?' 'Why do you lay this burden on me?' 'Did I conceive these people?' 'Why am I a nursing mother to them?' 'Am I responsible for getting them to Egypt?' 'How can I provide meat for so many?' 'Lord, this burden is too great for me.' 'I'd rather die now than go on like this' (11-15).

Moses was depressed, irritable and resentful. He poured it all out before the Lord. It was a prayer born of frustration and anger. He was angry with his ungrateful congregation and he was angry with God. Why did the Lord leave it all to him? After all, it was God's plan to bring the Israelites from Egypt to Canaan. He had gone along with it because God commanded him. But now it was all too much. Worn out with listening to the people's whining and not sure of what God would do next, Moses had had enough. He blamed the Lord for giving him a burden he couldn't carry and he wanted to die.

But God answered Moses graciously! He understood the frustration, the petulance, the lack of faith and the rebellious spirit that blamed God for it all. He provided Moses with seventy elders who eased the burden of leadership (vv.16,17). He sent an east wind that brought quails into the camp and provided meat for them (vv.31,32). In grace and mercy God 'overlooked' the faults of Moses and sent him help and refreshment. In our deepest disappointments, God understands. In our frustrations, God is merciful. When we lash out at circumstances and even at God himself, He does not answer in kind. In our deepest discouragement, His love and grace and understanding are with us still.

67. Prevenient Grace

At first glance this passage seems to say that God is arbitrary in His judgements. To some people He will be gracious and merciful and to others He will not. God may act in mercy or in judgement, in love or in punishment, and He doesn't tell us why. We cannot question God's actions because He works according to His own purposes and He does not explain His ways. If He is merciful to individuals or to nations, it is because He willed it that way. Likewise if He punishes individuals or nations that is also the consequence of His secret counsels. When these words from Exodus are quoted by Paul in Romans 9, Calvinistic scholars and commentators have used them to support a doctrine of election. God has decreed to save some men and women while others are likewise decreed to damnation. So we are faced with a doctrine of God's irreversible and predestined plans.

When, however, these words are looked at carefully in their context, a very different interpretation emerges. The previous chapter records how Israel provoked the Lord to anger by their idolatry. From their golden rings and ornaments they forged an image of a molten calf and began to worship it (32:1-6). God's response was swift and decisive. He said to Moses, 'Let me alone, that my wrath may burn hot against them and I may consume them' (32:10). Although Israel was God's chosen people, dramatically rescued from Egyptian slavery, God was now going to destroy them and raise up a new nation from Moses' family (32:10). This shows very clearly that God's plan in choosing Israel to be His people was dependent on their obedience and loyalty. Moses prayed to God to spare the people and 'the Lord repented of the evil he thought to do' (32:14). Moses reprimanded the Israelites for the 'great sin' they had committed (32:30) and although God did not inflict the judgement He had threatened, yet the consequences of the idolatry were severe. God commanded Moses to lead the people into Canaan but warned that His Presence would no longer be with them. 'I will send an angel before you …but I will not go up among you, lest I consume you in the way, for you are a stiff-necked people' (33:2.3). Until now God Himself had been in the midst of His people, leading,

185

guiding and protecting them. But their rebellion and idolatry were such that God's righteous anger was likely to consume them, so God withdrew His Presence and sent an angel to lead them.

This solemn event tells us much about God's ways and purposes. God cannot live with His people's rebellion for His holy nature cannot excuse sin. God's purposes in election are not fixed and irreversible; His choice of Israel depended on their obedience. Moses was alarmed and fearful of what might happen if the Lord was no longer with them. God had commanded him to lead the people but had not told him who would go with them (v.12). He asked God to show him the divine plan 'that I may know you and find favour in your sight' (v.13). Moses' prayer was to know God's ways. What did God intend for His people? Would He keep His promises and bring them into Canaan as He had promised? How could Moses be sure that he himself was pleasing to God?

God immediately responded to Moses' prayer with a great promise. 'My presence will go with you and I will give you rest' (v.14). God had threatened to remove his presence from Israel but now He revokes the threat and promises to be with His people. What a clear assurance this is that God listens to His people when they pray earnestly. Moses had cried out to God not to leave His people and God answered affirmatively. No doubt emboldened by this wonderful promise, Moses had one last request to make. 'Show me your glory' (v.18). The word for 'glory' is *kabod*, meaning the indescribable, ineffable, unutterable glorious presence of YHWH. But mortal eyes cannot look on God until He comes in human flesh in Jesus Christ (John 14:9). Even Moses can only see where God has passed by and know Him by what He has done (vv.21-23).

All through the Bible we learn that God is holy and that all mankind is sinful. If there is to be forgiveness for our sins and if we are to be reconciled to God, then a way must be found to bridge the gap between the divine holiness and human sin. And God Himself has bridged that gap by what Scripture repeatedly calls God's grace. As early as

Genesis 6 we read that Noah 'found favour (grace) in the eyes of the Lord' (v.8). God's grace is not just some kind of influence, some kind of heavenly ether that floats in the atmosphere. God's grace is His loving disposition, His loving kindness to mankind. God's grace is revealed in all His mercy, all His kindness, all His interventions and actions in human history. In particular His deliverance and preservation of His people Israel are demonstrations of His grace. It was, however, in the coming of His Son Jesus Christ that the world saw the greatest demonstration of God's grace to sinners. As Paul wrote, 'The grace of God has appeared for the salvation of all men' (Titus 2:11). It is 'by grace' that we have been saved through faith (Eph. 2:8).

All God's dealing with humanity spring from His grace. Although our sins separate us from God, in His grace He makes provision for our redemption. What is recorded in Exodus 33 is a clear revelation of God's wonderful grace. Israel's sinful rebellion and idolatry deserved judgement but God graciously spared them when they repented. This divine grace is a manifestation of God's character and it always precedes our repentance. Theologians call this grace 'prevenient grace' (from the Latin *praevenire*, meaning 'go before') because it 'goes before' our repentance and sorrow for sin. It is God's prevenient grace that prompts us and enables us to turn to God in repentance. When God told Moses that He would reveal to him His name, He meant that He would show him the Divine nature. Then He added, 'I will be gracious to whom I will be gracious and will show mercy on whom I will show mercy' (v.19). God acts in grace and mercy to all who repent of their sin and earnestly seek His forgiveness. No such promise is made to those who harden their hearts and who refuse God's offer of mercy. His 'graciousness,' meaning His grace, is directed to all who humbly confess their sin, and to all these He shows mercy. This wonderful disclosure of God's name, that is, God's nature, as grace and mercy, is reinforced in the next chapter. 'The Lord passed before him and proclaimed, "The Lord, the Lord, a God merciful and gracious, slow to anger and abounding in steadfast love and faithfulness"' (34:6). In a hymn dealing with how God's universal

love and mercy are demonstrated in the death of Christ, Charles
Wesley wrote:

> 'Tis Love! 'tis Love! Thou diedst for me
> I hear Thy whisper in my heart
> The morning breaks, the shadows flee
> Pure, universal Love thou art;
> To me, to all, Thy mercies move
> Thy nature and Thy name is Love.

68. A Tongue In Every Wound

These words come from the eloquent oration of Mark Antony for the murdered Julius Caesar in Shakespeare's play of that name. Brutus, Cassius, Casca and the other conspirators believe the people of Rome will support their treachery but that was before Antony's speech. Antony begins his oration in low key, saying he has not come to praise Caesar, just to bury him. He reminds the citizens of Rome of all that Caesar did for them. Was Caesar ambitious for his own glory? Brutus says he was and, adds Antony, we all know 'that Brutus is an honourable man.' Four times Antony speaks of Brutus' honour and with each mention of it the tension rises in the crowd. Soon Antony has the people crying out for vengeance on Caesar's enemies. As they hang on his every word, he declaims with unsurpassed dramatic eloquence: 'I show you sweet Caesar's wounds and bid them speak for me. But were I Brutus, and Brutus Antony, there were an Antony would ruffle up your spirits and put a tongue in every wound of Caesar, that should move the stones of Rome to rise and mutiny.'

A tongue in every wound! As Antony stands by the bloodied body of the murdered Caesar he declares that every wound, made by the traitors' swords, cries out for justice. The murderers have been exposed! Their crime is plain for all to see! Antony had made the wounds of Caesar speak! He put a tongue in every wound!

Charles Wesley, in a great hymn on Christ's heavenly intercession, did likewise with the wounds of Jesus. The believer can have perfect confidence. Not only has Christ died and risen but now He intercedes.

> Arise, My soul, arise,
> Cast off thy guilty fears
> The bleeding sacrifice
> In my behalf appears.
> Before the Throne my Surety stands
> My name is written on His hands.
>
> Five bleeding wounds He bears
> Received on Calvary...

Julius Caesar, too, had bleeding wounds, and in every one a 'tongue' cried out. Their cry was for vengeance, for retribution; murder must be atoned for. But the wounds of Jesus cry out, not for vengeance but for forgiveness, for mercy, for pardon!!

'Forgive him, O, forgive,' they cry
'Nor let that ransomed sinner die.'

What love! What grace! What a gospel! He who prayed for His enemies while He hung on the Cross now prays for you and me! 'My name,' the hymns tells us, 'is written on His hands.' He knows us! He loves us! He prays for us! A tongue in His every wound pleads on our behalf. And then Charles Wesley comes to the climax of his oration. God accepts the great redemption accomplished by His dear Son. We can know and be assured of our acceptance in Him!

The Father hears Him pray
His dear Anointed One
He cannot turn away
The presence of His Son.
The Spirit answers to the blood
And tells me I am born of God.

69. The Girl Without A Name

The early chapters of 2 Kings recount the death of the prophet Elijah and how he was succeeded by another prophet, Elisha. These were difficult times both in Israel and Judah. There was an uneasy peace between the two Hebrew kingdoms and both were threatened by hostile neighbours, especially Syria. A delightful story of a Hebrew slave girl is told in 2 Kings 5 and is set in the context of war. On Israel's northern border the Syrians had been strengthening their army and we are introduced to the Syrian commander, Naaman. He had a growing reputation as a successful soldier and even the Israelite historian describes him as 'a mighty man of valour' (2 Kings 5:1). But he was also a leper. That dreaded disease would have meant that Naaman had little personal contact with his family or the soldiers he commanded. Then a young Israelite girl is introduced in the story. She had been captured by the Syrians on one of their raids in Israel and she was given to Naaman's wife as a servant. This girl, for whom no name is given, saw the pain and distress caused in the family by Naaman's leprosy and she proposed a remedy. Although she was now living in Syria, she had not forgotten her homeland or her religion. In particular she knew that in Israel there was a prophet called Elisha, a true man of God. She had often heard of the miracles that Elisha performed, particularly the miracle of raising from death the son of the Shunammite woman (2 Kings 4:18-3).

Finally the girl plucked up courage and said to Naaman's wife, 'If my lord were with the prophet who is in Samaria he would soon be healed.' It was certainly a statement of faith! She was confident that Elisha, the true prophet of God, could do what all the medical skill available in Syria could not do. Eventually Naaman arrived at Elisha's door and the prophet, through a messenger, directed him to dip in the River Jordan seven times. When he eventually did, he was instantly healed of his leprosy. His testimony was, 'Now I know there is no God in all the earth but in Israel' (5:1). He even requested that he should be given two sacks of Israelite earth to take back to Syria. He knew that when he returned home his duties included going with his king into the pagan temple of Rimmon. When he knelt in that pagan temple, in spirit he would be kneeling before the one true God, the God of Israel. So Naaman was cured of his leprosy, and committed himself in his heart to Israel's God. It all came about because the Israelite girl had not forgotten her God and was enthusiastic to bear witness to her faith in the house of her owners. Let's encourage our children and young people in their Christian faith.

70. Determinism

Determinism is the philosophical doctrine that all the events of history, including all human actions, are fully determined by preceding events and consequently human freedom is an illusion. When determinism is talked about in Christian theology, it means that God has determined all events and no human action or prayer can alter what God has decreed. This understanding of God's ways gave rise to the doctrine of predestination, first introduced into Christian theology by Augustine of Hippo, North Africa, in the 5th century. This teaching was further refined by John Calvin in the 16th century and since that time theological determinism is usually called Calvinism. Calvin taught that before God created the human race, He predestined some men and women to eternal life and left the rest to be eternally condemned. Calvin further taught that God's decree of predestination is hidden in God's secret counsels and we cannot know why God acted like this. Thus the Calvinistic doctrine of predestination is theological determinism. All men and women are born into the world with their eternal destiny, either to salvation or damnation, already irrevocably fixed. Consequently Christ died only for the elect, those whom God has secretly elected to be saved.

In the 18th century John Wesley (1703-1791) reacted strongly against this Calvinistic teaching. He taught that God loved the world and that Christ died for all peoples. This means that all who obey the gospel call can be saved. Wesley explained that the Bible teaches that predestination means that God has decreed that all who believe in Christ will be saved and all who reject Christ will be lost. In His foreknowledge God has always known who will repent and believe in Christ and who will not. God *knows* this but He has not *predetermined* it. This Wesleyan teaching is sometimes called Arminianism, after the Dutch theologian, James Arminius (1560-1609). John Wesley founded Methodism and so Wesleyan teaching is found in Methodism and in the churches and denominations of the Holiness Movement that emerged in the 19th century. Christians of Wesleyan persuasion are not determinists. They believe that Christ died for all and that all who repent and believe in Christ as Saviour and Lord will be saved. Wesleyans stress that God has full knowledge of all events, past, present and future. In theology this is termed God's omniscience and it includes foreknowledge. God knows all events before they take place. Unlike determinists who say that God predestined some people to be saved and others to be lost, Wesleyans believe that God foreknows our response to the gospel but He did not predestine our response.

This important distinction between foreknowledge and foreordination is clearly illustrated in Isaiah 25. The chapter opens with praise to God for the great things He has done (vv.1-5). He has been a 'stronghold to the poor ...and the needy... a shelter from the storm and a shade from the heat' (v.4). Then verses 6-9 describe a great banquet that God has prepared for His people. The words 'on this mountain' (v.6) refer to Mount Zion in Jerusalem, but 'Jerusalem' is used to mean, not the city in Israel, but the final 'New Jerusalem' described in Revelation 21 and 22. For this reason commentators refer to Isaiah 25 as an eschatological vision (from the Greek *eschatos*, 'last,' hence eschatology, the study of the 'last times,' meaning the end of the world). The descriptions found in this chapter refer to God's final victory over all His enemies. The words 'He will swallow up death for ever' (v.8) are quoted in 1 Cor. 15:54, and the promise that 'the Lord God will wipe away tears from all faces' is cited in Rev. 21:4. In this New Jerusalem the redeemed say, 'Lo, this is our God, we have waited for him, that he might save us; let us be glad and rejoice in his salvation' (v.9).

Immediately after this glorious vision of all God's people gathered forever in His presence, there comes a solemn word of judgment. 'Moab shall be trodden down in his place, like straw is trodden down in a dung-pit' (v.10). Moab was a nation bordering Israel and became one of Israel's implacable enemies. The Moabites denied the Israelites passage through their country when they were about to enter Canaan (Judges 11:17), and the Moabite king, Balak, tried to put a curse on them (Numbers 22-24). After Israel finally settled in Canaan, the

Moabites attacked them many times (2 Kings 13:20, etc.). So 'Moab' became a word to describe the enemies of the Lord and His people. Here in Isaiah's great vision, all God's enemies, i.e. Moab, are excluded forever from God's presence. Why did this happen? Why did judgment fall on Moab? Had God foreordained that they should be punished?

The answer to these questions is found in a number of Old Testament passages. Isaiah says that God will 'lay low' Moab's pride (25:11). The Moabites gloried in their military might and success and this bred arrogance and contempt for other nations, especially Israel. Many of the references to Moab in the Old Testament speak of Moab's pride. 'We have heard of the pride of Moab, how proud he was; of his arrogance, his pride and his insolence' (Is. 16:6). Jeremiah speaks of God's judgments against Moab. 'You trusted in your own strongholds and your treasures' (48:7). 'We have heard of the pride of Moab; he is very proud; of his loftiness, his pride and his arrogance, and the haughtiness of his heart. I know his insolence, says the Lord' (Jer. 48:29,30). 'As I live, says the Lord, Moab shall become like Sodom... this shall be their lot in return for their pride, because they scoffed and boasted against the people of the Lord of hosts' (Zeph. 2:9, 10).

These references show that the Moabites had become a byword for pride, insolence and arrogance. They contemptuously derided the Lord's people and attacked them on every possible occasion. So in Isaiah's vision of the New Jerusalem, all 'Moabites' are excluded. This is not because God willed their exclusion, or determined their exclusion or decreed their exclusion. Instead all 'Moabites' exclude themselves from God's kingdom by stubbornly persisting in their pride and vanity and arrogantly refusing to repent and humble themselves before God.

71. Who Were They?

Athanasius (296-373AD). This is the name behind the Athanasian Creed. He was born into a prosperous family in Alexandria in Egypt, studied in the Christian school there and entered the ministry. He was twenty- nine years old when he accompanied Alexander, the bishop of Alexandria, to the Churches first ecumenical Council at Nicaea in 325AD. Although he could not take part in the Council's debates because he was a deacon and not a bishop, Alexander consulted him on the meaning of biblical texts and theological distinctions. With Emperor Constantine sitting as President, three hundred bishops argued about the Person of Christ. How is He the Son of God? Is He God or man or both together? Did He exist before He was born? If we worship Him does that mean we are worshipping two Gods? The young Athanasius was that some bishops wanted to impose the teaching of Arius on the Church. Arius was a popular preacher in Alexandria who taught that Christ was not eternal but was a 'Saviour' created by the Father. Athanasius worked with his bishop, Alexander, in framing what became known as the Nicene Creed. Our Lord's full divinity was safeguard in the words, 'eternally begotten of the Father, God from God, light from light, true God from true God, begotten, nor made, of one substance with the Father.'

When Bishop Alexander died in 328AD, Athanasius succeeded him as Bishop by popular demand. For the next forty-five Athanasius' devotion, scholarship and forceful lead ship established the Nicene Creed in the Christian Church. His enemies, both in Church and state, conspired against him and he was exiled five times from the See of Alexandria and spent a total of seventeen years in flight and hiding. It was his uncompromising stand for Nicene theology that gave rise to the familiar saying, Athanasius contra mundum, 'Athanasius against the world.' His name will always be linked with the triumph of New Testament Christology over every form of reductionism. Of his many writings the most significant was the great study on the person and work of Christ; On the Incarnation of the Word of God, written before he was thirty years old. The whole Church of Christ is always in need of bishops, leaders and theologians in the mould of Athanasius.

72. The 5 Minute Meditation

Paul's letter to the Philippian Christians is often called his letter of joy. He thanks God every time he prays for these Christians and he prays for them with joy (1:3,4). At their conversion God 'began a good work' in them and Paul knows that God will bring this work 'to completion at the day of Jesus Christ' (1:6). For the Philippians and for all Christians the work of salvation begins at the moment of conversion but it will continue throughout our lives. Then in Phil. 3:21 Paul speaks about the glorious hope of Christ's Second Coming when our earthly bodies will be transformed into our resurrection bodies. Our Lord will accomplish this by the 'power' or 'working' by which he will subdue all creation unto himself. That will be salvation completed, as Paul promised in the opening verses.

So in chapter 1 it is salvation begun and in chapter 3 it is salvation finished. But there is one more reference to this great work of salvation. In Phil 2:12, 13 Paul encourages these Christians to 'work out their own salvation.' This doesn't mean 'working for' our salvation but it certainly means 'working from' our salvation. All that God is doing in us by his grace and Holy Spirit is to be 'worked out' in everyday living. And then Paul adds a wonderful word of encouragement. We are able, or rather enabled, to 'work out' this salvation because 'God is at work in you' (3:13). Just think of it! The God who began our salvation and who promises that it will be completed is at work in each of us now! He has redeemed us! He owns us! He possesses us! And he is at work in us! He indwells us! Our little lives have become the dwelling place of the Lord God Almighty! Time and time again in his letters Paul writes about how Christians are 'in Christ' and Christ is 'in' us. He opens this Philippian letter by writing to the saints who are 'in Christ' (1:1). Likewise the Ephesian believer are 'in Christ' (Eph. 1:1). He assures the Colossian Christians that Christ is 'in' them as the hope of glory (1:27).

Why does Christ indwell his people? Why does he send his Spirit into our hearts as he promised his disciples (John 14:17)? Paul gives us the answer in Phil. 2:13. God is at work in you, he says, 'both to will and to work for his good pleasure.' Think of it! God gives us his Spirit both to <u>make us willing</u> and to <u>enable us to do</u> God's good pleasure. He initiates both the desire and the doing, the willing and the working, the aspiration and the achievement, the vision and the victory. Without him we can do nothing but by his indwelling Spirit all his plans for us will be fulfilled. What an encouragement! God hasn't finished with us yet! He's still working in us! He has given us his Holy Spirit! And he will bring us finally to completion, to resurrection, to glory and to be with him forever! And that is surely worth mediating on!

73. A Child Shall Lead Them

Ishmael & Isaac: The story of these two half-brothers is found very early in the Bible, in Genesis 17 and 21. Abraham was their father but while Isaac was Sarah's, Abraham's wife, son, Ishmael was the son of Sarah's maid, Hagar. God had promised Abraham and Sarah that they would have children but after many years they were still childless. Sarah than suggested that Abraham should have children by her maid Hagar and as soon as Hagar was pregnant, the trouble started. Sarah was jealous of Hagar and forced Abraham to send her away. God protected Hagar and told her to return to Abraham's house. There her son Ishmael was born and God promised that he would be the progenitor of a great nation (17:20). Some years later Abraham had a son by Sarah, Isaac, and the tensions in Abraham's home became unbearable. Ishmael mocked Isaac and Sarah again demanded that Hagar and her son should be sent away. God provided for Hagar and Ishmael in the wilderness and renewed His promise that Ishmael would be the father of a mighty nation.

Ishmael and Isaac grew up in a divided home. Abraham tried to keep the peace between his wife Sarah and her maid Hagar but conflict was inevitable. Instead of waiting for God's promise to be fulfilled, Abraham and Sarah short-circuited God's plan and Abraham had a son by Hagar. The two mothers despised each other and Ishmael was jealous when Isaac was born. Both sons were to have significant destinies. Ishmael became the father of the Arab nations while Isaac became the father of the nation of Israel. Down the long centuries, and at the present time, the conflict between Jews and Arabs is a constant reminder of how it all began. Abraham and Sarah failed to wait for God's promise to be realised and so Hagar and Ishmael enter the story. The two half-brothers grew up in a home full of tension, suspicion, bitterness and hatred – and the legacy continues to this day. Parents should learn from this Genesis story that their children are likely to reflect the values of the home into which they are born and the example with which they grow up.

74. On the Damascus Road

St Augustine of Hippo (354-430AD) is generally recognised as one of the greatest thinkers, theologians and bishops the Church has ever had. Not to be confused with the later Augustine of Canterbury, Augustine was born in Thagaste (modern Algiers) in North Africa and brought up in a home where his mother Monica was a devout Christian. His father was a pagan for most of his life. Augustine was a bright boy who did excellently at his local school and then went on to advanced studies in the great Christian centre, Carthage. It was there, however, as an enquiring teenager that he fell in with worldly companions and began to sample forbidden fruit. He lived with a girl by whom he had a son, much to his mother's grief. During these years, he confessed later, he was captivated by the love of learning, the lusts of the flesh and pride in his academic success. Later he moved to Rome, then to a professorship in Milan. There he began to attend the cathedral where Bishop Ambrose was the preacher. His mother Monica followed him to Italy and continued to pray constantly for her son's conversion.

When Jesus spoke with Nicodemus he said that the moving of the Spirit is like the wind and we don't know where it comes from or where it is going. Monica hoped that Ambrose's preaching would be the means of Augustine's conversion and certainly Augustine greatly admired Ambrose and found him a godly man and his intellectual equal. But the wind of the Spirit blew from an unexpected quarter. On an August Sunday in 386AD Augustine was visiting a friend's home in Milan. In his *Confessions*, his later-written autobiography, he tells us that as he walked in the garden that Sunday he heard the sound of children's voices as they played games in a neighbour's garden. He thought he heard the words *tolle legge, tolle legge*, which meant 'Take up and read.' He walked into the summer house, picked up a Latin Bible and it fell open at Romans 13:12. 'The night is far gone, the day is at hand. Let us cast off the works of darkness and put on the armour of light.' Augustine believed and in that moment he was converted to a living, vital faith in Christ as Lord and Saviour. There was no light shining from heaven or the audible voice of God as in Paul's experience but it was Augustine's Damascus Road. The wind of the Spirit transformed the proud and ambitious academic and in the years to come he would emerge as the greatest Father and theologian of the Early Church.

75. 666 and 777!!

The Revd Samuel Chadwick (1860-1932) was born in Burnley and went on to be one of the greatest preachers in Methodism. He attended Didsbury College, Manchester, and then entered the ministry at Edinburgh, Clydebank and then came to Oxford Place, Leeds, and stayed there thirteen years and filled the place every Sunday with his preaching. He was inspirational in preaching about the book of Revelation and one of his sermons, delivered at Hednesford in the Cannoch Circuit, caused such emotion that the men and women called out, 'Go on, go on.' The sermon was Rev. 13:18; 'And his number is six hundred, threescore and six.' It is called 'Sixes And Sevens,' and it was so popular that it was Chadwick's best ever.

The beast is not one but three. The first beast is the 'great red dragon' of chapter twelve. He has seven heads and ten horns and seven crowns upon his heads and was proclaimed in the earth. The second beast riseth up out of the sea and it is part leopard, bear, lion and has ten horns of Daniel's 'dreadful and terrible' beast. The third beast rises out of the earth and in many respects differs from its fellow beast. This miracle-working beast works in the intellect, will, hearts and conscience and shows such great signs and they almost deceive the very elect. John says: 'Here is wisdom: Let him that hath understanding count the number of the beast; for it is the number of a man; and his number is, Six hundred and threescore and six.' (13:18). The numbers are signs and must not be taken, in their or numerical value but in their symbolic sense. Six is nearer seven but always falls one short of completeness. If we wrote the number of the Trinity in figures, it would be 777. The Father, Son and Holy Ghost are each represented by the perfect number. The number of the beast, the trinity of evil, is 666, each beast having great authority and great power, but each falling short of completeness by one count. His number is 666. And the number of the beast is the number of a man, not the number of some individual; but just as in Rev. 21:17, 'the measure of a man,' means 'human' measure as distinct from angelic, so here is man as representation of his kind and the highest point to which to which humanity can reach. Such is identical is 666 and the highest possible of attainment, apart from God, in 666. This is Christ's method and the Kingdom can be reached by no other. His converting grace will change the and the host of hovel into a home and sweep away the dens of pestilence and death. His Spirit will quicken the faculties and make men and women eager to grow in knowledge and grace. He will reconstruct society individual and the host of Christian workers, despised preachers of the gospel and the old-fashioned who still go to prayer meetings are, after all, the best social reformers this world has. They have one complete Gospel; all the rest but 666.

Apply this to your own life. What is your number? Is it six or seven? You can get a good deal out of life of sixes. You may get a lot out of a life without religion. Given plenty of money, pleasant surroundings, brilliant companions, a man or women ought to be ashamed of himself if he cannot get a good time. Yet the best of the world's pleasures is only 6. The provoking thing is about is about it that there is always something short. It never quite satisfies. One day a fine specimen of the number 6 came to Jesus. He had kept the Commandments, he was greatly respected and when Jesus say him, he loved him. But he said to him. 'One thing you lack; sell all that you have and come follow me.' One thing you have – he represented number 6 – and he went away sorrowful.

When Chadwick returned home, he preached that sermon and he noticed a young man in his congregation. On Thursday he fell ill and on the Sunday morning the doctor pronounced him dying. At noon Chadwick was sent for and immediately he called on him to pray. The man called on him to sing, 'Jesus lover of my soul.' Then he looked up with a smile and said, 'I am going where there are no sixes; its 777!! Sing the Doxology.' Drawing his face close to Chadwick's, he whispered, 'It's 777'!!! In twenty minutes he was dead. His soul has passed beyond and his last words were, 'It's 777'!!!

76. John Wesley – Preacher of the Gospel

In this tercentenary year of John Wesley's birth there are books and articles being published, and conferences and seminars planned that are dealing with every aspect of his life and work. In this context it is very appropriate that the *Preacher's Magazine* should look at John Wesley the preacher. Dr A Skevington Wood, in his excellent study of John Wesley, *The Burning Heart: John Wesley Evangelist*, argues very convincingly that, first and foremost, Wesley was an evangelist. An evangelist is a herald, a preacher of the gospel, and Wesley took up this calling deliberately and gave himself to it with passion and dedication for the greater part of his life. He preached his first sermon on October 3rd, 1725, two weeks after his ordination as a deacon, and he preached his last sermon on February 23rd, 1791. Between these two dates he had given almost 66 years to preaching the gospel across the four kingdoms of England, Scotland, Ireland and Wales. He had also spent two years of ministry in Georgia and made two preaching visits to Holland in later life.

The years 1737 and 1738 were epochal years in John Wesley's life. Under the influence of the Moravians, first in Georgia and then in London, Wesley was coming to an understanding of salvation by faith that would not only transform his personal spiritual life but also revolutionise his preaching. The Aldersgate 'heart-warming' of May 24th, 1738, not only gave Wesley the assurance of his acceptance with God but it also gave him a new evangel. Eighteen days after the Aldersgate experience, Wesley preached at St Mary's, Oxford. His theme was 'Salvation by Faith' and it marked the beginning of half a century of gospel preaching. Compared with his earlier Oxford sermons, not only does this sermon declare the Pauline doctrine of salvation by faith far more clearly and unequivocally than they did, but there is also about it an urgency and an evangelistic thrust that marks Wesley's subsequent preaching. When John Wesley compared his earlier and later preaching, he pointed to his great discovery of salvation by faith.

From the year 1725 to 1729 I preached much, but saw no fruit to my labour. Indeed it could not be that I should; for I neither laid the foundation of repentance, nor of believing the gospel.... From the year 1729 to 1734, laying a deeper foundation of repentance, I saw a little fruit. But it was only a little; and no wonder: For I did not preach faith in the blood of the covenant. From 1734 to 1738, speaking more of faith in Christ, I saw more fruit of my preaching... From 1738 to this time, speaking continually of Jesus Christ, laying him only for the foundation of the whole building.... The word of God ran as fire among stubble.... multitudes crying out, 'What must I do to be saved?'

Monday, April 2nd, 1739 marked another important milestone in John Wesley's preaching ministry. At four in the afternoon that day he consented, in his own words, to be 'more vile' and preached to about three thousand people in a brickyard in Bristol. This open-air preaching, which Wesley always called 'field-preaching,' had been pioneered by George Whitefield but John Wesley was to make it his life's work. His theme that day in Bristol was near-prophetic, 'The Spirit of the Lord is upon me, because he has anointed me to preach the gospel'. Fifty-one and a half years later, Wesley preached his last open-air sermon, under an ash tree at Winchelsea on the south coast of England, from the words of Mark 1:15, 'Repent and believe the gospel.' In the years between the sermon in the brickyard and the sermon under the ash tree, Wesley had preached about forty-five thousand times and about 80% of that amazing ministry was conducted out-of-doors. In all places, in all weathers, to crowds large and small, he proclaimed the Good News across the four kingdoms of Great Britain for half a century. He preached in fields, in barns, on hillsides, at market crosses, in town and city streets. This tercentenary appreciation of John Wesley as a preacher will seek to answer two questions. First, what was the content of John Wesley's half-century of evangelistic preaching, and, second, what impression did Wesley's preaching make on his hearers?

What was the evangel that Wesley preached so effectively? We have already seen that he designated 1738 as the year in which the word of

God began to 'run as fire among stubble,' with multitudes crying out for salvation. 1738 was the year he 'discovered' the doctrine of salvation by faith in personal experience and the year in which it became his evangel. Wesley published some one hundred and forty sermons and the first impression on reading them is that they are theologically 'heavy' and surely not fitted for the unchurched masses who crowded to hear him preach. Wesley's published sermons are sprinkled with Greek and Latin quotations and with many citations from the English classical poets. Would the farm labourers of Lancashire, the cloth weavers in Yorkshire and the tin miners in Cornwall have understood such theologically orientated sermons?

The answer is simple – they didn't have to! John Wesley did *not* preach these sermons as they appeared in print. He published the sermons to inform his Methodist people, and whoever else might read them, about what the doctrines of Methodism were. When the sermons are looked at carefully it is important to note that most of them are intended to build up in holy faith those who are already converted. Certainly there are sermons like 'Salvation by Faith' (1738), 'The Almost Christian' (1741), 'Justification by Faith' (1746) and 'The New Birth' (1760), that are intended to bring sinners to saving faith but such sermons are a minority in the collection. The majority of the published sermons are directed to those who are already Christians and Wesley's intention is to build them up in faith and holiness. There are 13 sermons based on 'The Sermon on the Mount' and many sermons on practical daily Christian living. These include sermons like 'Self Denial,' 'The Cure of Evil Speaking,' 'The Use of Money,' 'The Danger of Riches,' 'On Family Religion,' 'On Temptation,' 'The Duty of Reproving our Neighbour,' and many other practical and ethical subjects.

If John Wesley did not preach these sermons in his half-century of evangelism, what did he preach? The answer to this is found in a manuscript that Wesley entitled 'The Sermon Register.' It details the dates, locations and sermon texts for fourteen years of his ministry, from January 1747 to December 1761. Almost certainly Wesley had kept a sermon register for his entire ministry but the records for the other years are lost. This register, covering almost a third of his itinerant ministry, is the best guide we have to the sermons he preached across the kingdoms.

The same texts are used scores of times as Wesley travelled from place to place, and, on closer examination, a list of favourite texts begins to emerge. The texts that he preached from again and again include the following. 'What is a man profited if he shall gain the whole world and lose his own soul'? (Matt. 16:26); 'Repent and believe the gospel' (Mk. 1:15); 'Thou art not far from the kingdom of God' (Mk. 12:34); 'Joy shall be in heaven over one sinner that repenteth' (Lk. 15:7); 'Between us and you there is a great gulf fixed' (Lk. 16:26); 'It is God that justifieth' (Rom. 8:33); 'All things are of God who hath reconciled us to himself by Jesus Christ' (2 Cor. 5:18). Interestingly the one text from which John Wesley seems to have preached most often was, 'And the Spirit and the bride say, Come...' (Rev. 22:17).

These were the texts that Wesley used to convince his hearers that they were sinners, to warn them to flee from the wrath to come, to bring them to repentance and to lead them to saving faith in Christ. These sermons were not preached from written outlines or notes but straight from the biblical text. In many places in his *Journal* Wesley describes what his preaching was meant to do. 'I there offered Christ.' 'I offered the grace of God.' 'I offered the redemption that is in Christ Jesus.' 'I proclaimed the Name of the Lord.' 'I proclaimed Christ crucified.' 'I proclaimed free salvation.' 'I declared the free grace of God.' 'I exhorted the wicked to forsake his way.' 'I began to call sinners to repentance.' 'I invited all guilty, helpless sinners.' This was soul-saving preaching and the sermons had anecdotes, illustrations and stories that the common people could easily understand. John Wesley's favourite quotations from Latin authors and the English classical poets were not used in his field-preaching; rather he spoke straight from the heart in plain, pointed sentences that called sinners to repentance and directed them to faith in a crucified and risen Lord.

Having looked at the content and style of John Wesley's evangelistic preaching, the question is very relevant: what impression did this preaching make on those who heard him? Out of the thousands who were converted through his preaching a few left written records of their experiences, so we can call the witnesses. John Nelson was a stone-cutter by profession and he heard Wesley preach in Moorfields in London. 'As soon as he got upon the stand he stroked back his hair and turned his face towards where I stood His countenance struck such an awful dread upon me that it made my heart beat like the pendulum of a clock. I thought his whole discourse was aimed at me. When he had done I said, "This man can tell the secrets of my heart: he hath not left me there, for he hath showed me the remedy, even the blood of Jesus."'

Later Nelson became one of Wesley's itinerant preachers, as did Alexander Mather, who recorded: 'Wesley preached at West Street and under that sermon God set my heart at liberty, removing my sins from me as far as the east is from the west. My load was gone and I could praise God from the ground of my heart.' Thomas Tennant wrote to Wesley and described how his preaching had affected him. 'When I have heard you preach, I thought you appeared as with a sword in your hand, with which you cleft me asunder. At such times the word was indeed quick and powerful, piercing and wounding my inmost soul.' Silas Told was invited by a friend to hear Wesley preach. Told went unwillingly and Wesley preached on the forgiveness of sins. He wrote later, 'I had never heard this doctrine preached in the Church. I plainly saw I could never be saved without knowing my sins forgiven… Under this sermon my soul was filled with a hatred for sin, and also with zeal for the truth.'

These and other eye-witness accounts of John Wesley's preaching are very vivid. Wesley took an evangelistic text and applied the gospel with power and conviction. In the pulpit he warned against sin and damnation, he pleaded with men and women to repent and call upon the Lord and he applied the gospel promises with passion and sometimes with tears. Our last witness is Hester Ann Rogers, whose

Diary is a marvellous record of the spiritual life of one of the outstanding women of 18th century English Methodism. Among other treasures she gave a very full account of John Wesley preaching on the text, 'The kingdom of heaven is at hand.' Although Wesley did not ask penitents to stand up or raise their hands as a sign of spiritual need, clearly the sermon's conclusion was an invitation in its directness and simplicity.

> Yield now to him who loveth you, who died for you, who will save you from all your sins here and from Hell hereafter. He loves you all, even thou, poor sinner. He bled for thee, and wilt thou resist Him still? Dost thou feel thou art a sinner deserving nothing but hell? Fear not, look up, He is nigh thee. Look up now, even at this moment. 'Believe on the Lord Jesus Christ and thou shalt be saved.'... Come just as thou art. Come now a helpless sinner to a mighty Saviour. The kingdom of heaven is at hand! It is nigh thee, it is here, take it! Now believe, wait for nothing!

Then Mrs Rogers' account tells what happened.

> Mr Wesley prayed for penitents, for backsliders, for the unawakened and for children, such as could till now break the Sabbath, steal apples, tell lies and disobey parents. In short I never heard him so full of life and love. He wept several times while he prayed. All the congregation were in tears... As we came home in the chaise, Mr Wesley said, 'I never saw a more lovely congregation, Hetty. They were like melting wax; just fit for divine impressions. But God was with us, there's the secret.' Tears filled his eyes.

John Wesley was 79 years old when Hester Rogers heard him preach this sermon and in many ways, Wesley's whole preaching ministry is encapsulated in this stirring account. He chose a simple gospel text (Matt. 4:17) and he explained it and applied it to every heart. He warned, he exhorted, he invited, he pleaded, he prayed and he wept. And he gave the glory to God, for the secret of this soul-saving sermon, and thousands like it, was – 'God was with us.' In this tercentenary year of Wesley's birth we are reminded that above all else he was John Wesley – Preacher of the Gospel.

Other Books by Revd Dr Herbert Boyd McGonigle

William Cooke on Entire Sanctification, Beacon Hill Press, Kansas City, Missouri, 1978.

The Arminianism of John Wesley, Moorleys Print & Publishing, Ilkeston, Derbyshire, 1988.

John Wesley and the Moravians, Moorleys Print & Publishing, Ilkeston, Derbyshire, 1995.

John Wesley's Doctrine of Prevenient Grace, Moorleys Print & Publishing, Ilkeston, Derbyshire, 1995.

Scriptural Holiness: The Wesleyan Distinctive, Moorleys Print & Publishing, Ilkeston, Derbyshire, 1995.

Sufficient Saving Grace: John Wesley's Evangelical Arminianism, 350 pages, Paternoster Publishing, Carlisle, Cumbria, 2001.

To God Be The Glory: The Killadeas Convention 1952-2002, Moorleys Print & Publishing, Ilkeston, Derbyshire, 2002.

John Wesley's Arminian Theology: An Introduction, Moorleys Print & Publishing, Ilkeston, Derbyshire, 2005.

A Burning and a Shining Light: The Life and Ministry of William Bramwell, Moorleys Print & Publishing, Ilkeston, Derbyshire, 2009.

Christianity or Deism? John Wesley's Response to John Taylor's Denial of the Doctrine of Original Sin, Moorleys Print & Publishing, Ilkeston, Derbyshire, 2012.

John Wesley: Exemplar of the Catholic Spirit, Moorleys Print & Publishing, Ilkeston, Derbyshire, 2014.

Charles Wesley: For All, For All My Saviour Died, Moorleys Print & Publishing, Ilkeston, Derbyshire, 2014.

John Wesley: The Death of Christ, Moorleys Print & Publishing, Ilkeston, Derbyshire, 2014.

Epworth: The Cradle of Methodism, Moorleys Print & Publishing, Ilkeston, Derbyshire, 2014.

John Wesley: Doctrine of Final Judgement, Moorleys Print & Publishing, Ilkeston, Derbyshire, 2015.

Thomas Walsh: Saint and Scholar, Moorleys Print & Publishing, Ilkeston, Derbyshire, 2015.

Our Story: Autobiographical thoughts from the pen of Revd. Dr. Herbert B. McGonigle, Nazarene Theological College Archives, Manchester, 2015.

Dr. Adam Clarke: Methodist Preacher and Scholar, Moorleys Print & Publishing, Ilkeston, Derbyshire, 2015.

Gideon Ouseley: Methodist Preacher and Biblical Scholar, Moorleys Print & Publishing, Ilkeston, Derbyshire, 2015.

Thomas Cook: Evangelist and Saint, Moorleys Print & Publishing, Ilkeston, Derbyshire, 2016.

The Methodist Pentecost, 1758-1763, Moorleys Print & Publishing, Ilkeston, Derbyshire, 2016.

John Fletcher, Methodist Saint and Scholar, Moorleys Print & Publishing, Ilkeston, Derbyshire, 2016.

An Appreciation of Revd. Dr. John Henry Jowett's Heaven's Hallelujah, Moorleys Print & Publishing, Ilkeston, Derbyshire, 2016.

General William Booth, Moorleys Print & Publishing, Ilkeston, Derbyshire, 2016.

John Wesley on The Great Salvation, Moorleys Print & Publishing, Ilkeston, Derbyshire, 2017.

Samuel Chadwick: Preacher and Evangelist, Moorleys Print & Publishing, Ilkeston, Derbyshire, 2017.

Francis William Crossley, Moorleys Print & Publishing, Ilkeston, Derbyshire, 2018.

Dr. Alexander Maclaren: Preacher and Expositor, Moorleys Print & Publishing, Ilkeston, Derbyshire, 2018.

Herbert and Jeanne McGonigle: Our Story, Moorleys Print & Publishing, Ilkeston, Derbyshire, 2018.

Through the Year with John and Charles Wesley, Moorleys Print & Publishing, Ilkeston, Derbyshire, 2019.

2002 Didsbury Lecturers: John Wesley, Moorleys Print & Publishing, Ilkeston, Derbyshire, 2020.